KU-035-537

THE PATTEN FOUNDATION

Mr. Will Patten of Indianapolis (A.B., Indiana University, 1893) made, in 1931, a gift for the establishment of the Patten Foundation at his Alma Mater. Under the terms of this gift, which became available upon the death of Mr. Patten (May 3, 1936), there is to be chosen each year a Visiting Professor who is to be in residence several weeks during the year. The purpose of this prescription is to provide an opportunity for members and friends of the University to enjoy the privilege and advantage of personal acquaintance with the Visiting Professor. The Visiting Professor for the Patten Foundation in 1957 was

PROFESSOR AZIZ S. ATIYA

NOTE

This is a companion volume to
CRUSADE, COMMERCE AND CULTURE
published simultaneously by Indiana University Press

Contents

Preface   11

Abbreviations   15

CRUSADE HISTORIOGRAPHY / 17

MONUMENTAL COLLECTIONS / 29

   I. Recueil des Historiens des Croisades   29
  II. Palestine Pilgrims' Text Society Library   47
 III. Archives de l'Orient Latin   52
  IV. Exuviae Sacrae Constantinopolitanae   57
   V. Bibliothèque des Croisades   60
  VI. Records of Civilization   70
 VII. Bibliotheca Geographorum Arabicorum   73

GENERAL BIBLIOGRAPHY / 79

 I. Bibliography

    1. Western   79
    2. Arabic and Oriental   81

II. Chronography and Chronology

    1. Western and Crusading   84

2. Byzantine   84
3. Arabic and Oriental   85

III. Historical Background

1. European History   86
2. Rome and Papacy   86
3. Byzantium and the Byzantine Church   88
4. The Mediterranean   90
5. Mohammedanism, Muslim Peoples, and
   Ottoman History   91
6. Near Eastern Christianity   96

IV. The Crusade Movement

1. The Crusades and the Latin Orient   98
   Larger Works   99
   Special Encyclopedias and Dictionaries   99
   General History   99
   Background to Crusades   107
   Pilgrimage   109
   First Crusade   109
   Second Crusade   113
   Third Crusade   115
   Henry VI's Plan of Crusade   117
   Fourth Crusade   118
   Children's Crusade   122
   Fifth Crusade   122
   Sixth Crusade   124
   Seventh and Eighth Crusades   125
2. The Crusade in the Later Middle Ages   127
   Propagandists and Missionaries   127
   The Later Crusade   131
   Mongols and Missions   134
   Cyprus and the Crusade   136
3. Aftermath of the Crusades   138
   The Counter-Crusade   138
   Egypt and Syria   140

The Turkish Counter-Crusade 141
Constantinople 142
4. Romance Literature 143
5. Military Orders of Religion 143
General Works 143
The Templars 144
The Hospitallers—Rhodes and Malta 145
6. The Art of War 146
7. Islamic Culture 147
General Literature 147
Philosophy and Theology 149
Science and Mathematics 152
Astronomy and Astrology 153
Medicine 154
Arts and Architecture 155
Philology 156
Literature 156
Education 158
8. East-West Commerce 158
Trade 158
Mediterranean Shipping and Naval History 160
Arab Shipping and Naval History 161
Turkish Shipping and Naval History 161
9. Geography, Travel, and Atlases 162
Index 167

Preface

THE PURPOSE of this companion volume to *Crusade, Commerce and Culture* is twofold. First, there is the intention to supplement the historiographical and bibliographical information given in the text of the *Crusade* volume. Second, it is the author's hope that this may prove an initial step toward a complete and definitive bibliography of materials on the Crusade.

The wealth of material in this field—covering the Crusade in the early and later Middle Ages, its antecedents in Greco-Persian history, and its translation into the modern Eastern Question and today's Pan-Arab movement—makes definitive bibliography a monumental task. Moreover, the diversity of languages is great—sources being available in French, German, Italian, Spanish, Latin, Greek, Arabic, Turkish, and Slavonic tongues, as well as other linguistic variations.

The sources range themselves into two broad categories: published works and periodical literature (General Bibliography), and collections (Monumental Collections). In addition to selected materials in these two categories, a brief essay on the historiography of the Crusade has been supplied (Crusade Historiography), together with supplemental notes.

General bibliographies abound—none of them perfect but most of them valuable—with information for specialists in many areas: chronography, geography, diplomatic history, military history, literary history, commercial history, to name but a few. Among recent and excellent works worthy of special mention are A. Pearson's *Index Islamicus* (1958), H. Mayer's *Bibliographie zur Geschichte der Kreuzzüge* (1960) *, L. N. Malclès's *Les Sources du Travail —Bibliographies Spécialisées* (1952), and the American Historical Association's *Guide to Historical Literature* (1961).

However, in the area of Monumental Collections, a lacuna has long existed which greatly handicaps the research worker. Such works as the French *Recueil des Historiens des Croisades,* the Arabic *Bibliotheca Geographorum Arabicorum,* and others, require description and annotation, and the present volume has tried to fulfill this purpose.

The venture has of necessity been limited and selective, but it is hoped that the choices made will provide a starting point for additional interest and research. In time it is hoped that the contents of other collections will be described and analyzed—the *Monumenta Germaniae His-*

---

* This extensive bibliography appeared after the compilation of the material in this volume had been completed and sent to the printer. I have been able to make some use of it only while proofreading; and since our approaches are different, the two works must consequently fulfill services of a different character and continue to live together.

*torica,** the *Recueil des Historiens des Gaules et de la France,* the *Rolls Series,* and all the national archives and publications of the many nations and nationalities which participated in the Crusade. In the present volume significant publications which are not covered in the Monumental Collections section are mentioned in supplementary notes and in the various parts of the General Bibliography.

The author has designed this volume of historiography and bibliography so that more stress is laid upon Arabic literature and sources, an area relatively unexplored by research workers and writers. He has also arranged his materials to support his distinction between the Crusade and the Crusades. The Crusade is a movement with roots deep in the Greco-Persian-Arabic past, and with consequences extending far beyond the fall of Acre in 1291. The Crusades individually may be regarded as military ventures of a special character initiated by Urban II toward the end of 1095. It is the author's intention to demonstrate that the Crusades are only one phase of a vast and widespread Crusade Movement.

I am deeply indebted to friends and colleagues—too many to be enumerated—whose encouragement and support rendered both volumes a reality. Mrs. Constance R. Pitchell of the Indiana University Press has been my editorial advisor and she has spared no effort to rectify my failures. With the patience of a true medievalist, she undertook the tedious task of editing my manuscript, correcting my proofs, and compiling my indices. Mr. Thomas Glastras of the Reference Department of the Indiana University Library has never failed to answer our requests and help

---

* J. C. Anderssohn: *The Ancestry and Life of Godfrey of Bouillon,* Indiana University, Bloomington, Ind., made an initial attempt to signal the relevant contents of the *Monumenta,* but a definitive and detailed analysis remains to be done.

in solving some of our bibliographical problems. Miss Miriam S. Farley, the Managing Editor of the Press, has handled my text from the beginning with Mrs. Pitchell, and I have continuously availed myself of her wisdom. To all of them, I wish to express my personal appreciation. But responsibility for all shortcomings in both volumes must rest solely with the author.

AZIZ S. ATIYA

Middle East Center
University of Utah
December 4, 1961

Abbreviations

Acta—*Acta Sanctorum* (supplemented, with bibliography, by *Analecta Bollandiana*)

A.H.R.—*American Historical Review*

Archives—*Archives de l'Orient Latin*

C.H.R.—*Catholic Historical Review*

C.M.H.—*Cambridge Mediaeval History*

Corpus Script.—*Corpus Scriptorum Historiae Byzantinae*

Deutsche Geschichte—*Forschungen zur Deutsche Geschichte*

Doc. Inédits—*Collection de Documents Inédits sur l'Histoire de France*

E. de C.—*Bibliothèque de l'École des Chartes*

E.H.R.—*English Historical Review*

Gesta—*Gesta Dei Per Francos* (ed. Bongars)

Gibbon—E. Gibbon, *Decline and Fall of the Holy Roman Empire*

Golubovich—R.P.G. Golubovich, *Biblioteca Bio-Bibliografica della Terra Santa e dell' Oriente Francescano*

Hautes Études—*Bibliothèque de l'École des Hautes Études*

H.S.—Hakluyt Society

H.Z.—*Historisches Zeitschrift*

I.C.—*Islamic Culture*

J.A.—*Journal Asiatique*

J.S.—*Journal des Savants*

M.A.A.—Medieval Academy of America

Michaud—J. F. Michaud, *Bibliothèque des Croisades; Histoire des Croisades*

M.G.H.—*Monumenta Germaniae Historica*

Mon. et Mém.—*Monuments et Mémoires de l'Académie des Inscriptions et des Belles-Lettres*

Paetow—A. C. Paetow, *A Guide to the Study of the Middle Ages; The Crusades and Other Historical Essays, Presented to Dana C. Munro*

Patr. Gr.—*Patrologia Graeca* (ed. Migne)

Patr. Lat.—*Patrologia Latina* (ed. Migne)

Patr. Or.—*Patrologia Orientalis* (ed. Graffin and Nau)

Records—*Records of Civilization* (Columbia University)

Recueil—*Recueil des Historiens des Croisades*

Rev. Or. Lat.—*Revue de l'Orient Latin*

Rev. Belge—*Revue Belge Philosophique et Historique*

Rev. Écc.—*Revue Historique Écclesiastique*

R.H.—*Revue Historique*

R.H.E.—*Revue d'Histoire Écclesiastique*

R.H.G.F.—*Recueil des Historiens des Gaules et de la France*

R.H.R.—*Revue d'Histoire des Religions*

R.Q.H.—*Revue des Questions Historiques*

Rolls—*Rolls Series* (*Rerum Britannicarum medii aevi scriptores*, or *Chronicles and Memorials of Great Britain and Ireland during the Middle Ages;* popularly known as the *Rolls Series,* because published under the nominal direction of the Master of the Rolls)

Soc. Or. Lat.—Société de l'Orient Latin: 1. *Archives de l'Orient Latin;* 2. *Revue de l'Orient Latin;* 3. *Série Géographique;* 4. *Série Historique*

Crusade Historiography

PERHAPS NO OTHER SUBJECT in the annals of history has so captivated the imagination and given rise to such a tremendous literary output as the Crusades. Writers of many ages and countries have been attracted to this world movement ever since the first historian of the Crusades, Archbishop William of Tyre,* wrote his history of the holy war

* William of Tyre (the Arabic Ṣūr), is regarded as one of the most remarkable historians of the Middle Ages. Born in the East, he completed his education in France and Rome. Besides French and Latin, he was apparently acquainted with both Arabic and Greek. As archbishop of Tyre from 1160 and chancellor of the Latin kingdom of Jerusalem from 1170 to 1174, he had access to the archives of the Holy Sepulchre and he was familiar with the writings of eyewitnesses of previous events, such as Fulcher of Chartres, Albert of Aachen (Aix), Raymond of Aguilers, and Walter the Chancellor, as well as some versions of the "Gesta Francorum." He is said to have begun writing his history in 1169; and in 1183, on failing to secure preferment to the

in the twelfth century. The modern pioneers in this sphere were Wilken in Germany and Michaud in France, who published extensive Crusade histories in the first three decades of the last century.* Both valued the use of the sources, not only of the West but also of the East. Both realized that historians are judges of the past who, in order to declare a just verdict, must study carefully the evidence of plaintiffs, defendants, and witnesses. In the case of the Crusades, the parties were the East and the West, the peoples of Christian Europe versus those of the Islamic world, and the subject of litigation was possession of the Holy Land. Wilken appears to have been the more critical of the two authors, and he used more freely the scanty Oriental sources at his disposal in European languages. Michaud lapsed into the ways of journalism and misused an eloquent style in order to heighten the effect of romantic episodes upon the reader.

Nevertheless, we owe both classical writers a permanent debt of gratitude, not only for drawing attention to the importance of Oriental sources, but also for writing with affection and enthusiasm about the Middle Ages in general. Their predecessors from Thomas Fuller: *Historie of the Holy Warre*, 3rd ed., Cambridge 1647, to Johann C. L. Haken: *Gemälde der Kreuzzüge nach Palästina zur Befreiung des heiligen Grabes*, 4 pts., Frankfurt 1808–20—to-

---

patriarchate of Jerusalem, he retired to Rome, where he devoted the rest of his lifetime to the completion of his history until his death, probably in 1187, the year of the fall of the Holy City into Saladin's hands. The "Historia" covers Crusading events from 1095 to 1184, and has since been updated by several continuators. In spite of chronological and other imperfections, the work is a classic in the history of the Crusade and of the Franks of Outremer. (See Monumental Collections, section VI, for citation.)

* See below, General Bibliography, section IV. 1, for citation of these works.

gether with a host of other writers between them *—all
wrote in an aggressive tone against the Middle Ages in general and the Crusade in particular (a dark period of bar-
barous fanaticism and violence).

Meanwhile, a modest but felicitous beginning was made
in the editing of the original sources from hitherto unpublished manuscripts. Bongars may rightfully be regarded as
the pioneer in this movement. He published the monumental *Gesta Dei per Francos* at Hanover in 1611, a work of
high caliber for any age. The first volume includes several
chronicles of the First Crusade, and the second volume is
devoted chiefly to the *Secreta Fidelium Crucis* of Marino
Sanudo the Elder, a 14th-century Venetian noble of the
duchy of Naxos in the Aegean.**

Then, about the beginning of the eighteenth century,
the Benedictines of the Congrégation de Saint-Maur, famous for their literary activities, contemplated the publication of the entire range of sources of the history of the
Latin Orient. The task of collecting the Western chronicles
of the Crusade attained considerable progress even before
1740, and this material was made available in the pages of
the formidable *Histoire Littéraire de la France*. Subse-
quently, the authors envisaged the edition of the Oriental
texts related to Crusade history. This incalculable burden
was entrusted in 1770 to Dom Berthereau, professor of
Greek and Hebrew at the Abbey of Saint-Denis in Paris.
He set to work on the Arabic chronicles in manuscript at
the Bibliothèque du Roi and the library of Saint-Germain
de Près. Unfortunately, Dom Berthereau died in 1794, and

---

* Including Joseph de Guignes: *Histoire des Huns*, Paris 1756–58;
Jean Baptiste Mailly: *L'Esprit des Croisades*, 4 vols., Dijon 1780; and
F. W. Heller: *Geschichte der Kreuzzüge nach dem heiligen Lande*, 3
bde., Frankenthal und Mannheim 1816.

** See Atiya: *Crusade, Commerce and Culture*, ch. 3.

the work was further interrupted by the outbreak of the French Revolution.

With the return of peace, Michaud tried to revive these activities, though on a completely different basis, in his *Bibliothèque des Croisades,* four volumes appended to his three-volume *Histoire des Croisades,* first published in 1829. But instead of editing original texts, he translated masses of extracts relevant to the history of the Crusades from the sources preserved in various national collections. The first volume was derived from the chronicles of France, the second from those of Italy and England, the third from the chronicles of the Nordic countries and Greece and Turkey; and in the fourth volume Michaud was assisted by Reinaud in the translation of a selection of Arabic texts.

The work of the Benedictines was ultimately inherited by the Académie des Inscriptions et des Belles-Lettres, which formed a committee of five (Hase, Quatremère, Reinaud, Guérard, and Beugnot) to resume the work so auspiciously begun at Saint-Maur.* The result was, with all its faults and shortcomings, the greatest achievement to date in the service of the history of the Crusades. Under the general title *Recueil des Historiens des Croisades* was published a series of five volumes of historians of the West, four volumes from Arabic, two from Greek, two from Armenian, and two of laws.** It is to be noted that the contents of the legal volumes are derived from secondary registers and copies, since all the original charters and documents pertaining to administration, deposited in the Church of the Holy Sepulchre, were destroyed by fire or lost in the fray when Saladin stormed the city of Jerusalem in 1187. We have to add to these the *Assise de Romanie,*

---

* The work of the Benedictines and the Académie, in particular of M. Reinaud, is discussed further below, Monumental Collections, sections I and V.

** See below, Monumental Collections, section I.

as well as the *Assise d'Antioche*, published in Venice in 1875 and 1876 respectively.

Last but not least, we must acknowledge the magnificent work of the Société de l'Orient Latin, founded in 1875 by Comte Riant in Paris and Geneva, to complete the work of the Académie des Inscriptions and to fill the lacunae in the *Recueil* on a more scientific basis. Its publications contain four sets. The *Série Géographique* (5 vols.) includes unpublished itineraries of pilgrims and travellers to the Holy Land. The *Série Historique* (5 vols.) includes chronicles, correspondence, charters, and similar historical documents. In the *Archives de l'Orient Latin* (2 vols.) a great mass of variegated material is assembled; * while the *Revue de l'Orient Latin* (12 vols.) is open to all research in the field. Scholars like de Mas Latrie, Röhricht, Hagenmeyer, Kohler, Molinier, Schlumberger, and many others have been recruited for the work and have made splendid contributions to its progress. The result has been admirable both in quantity and in quality; but the death of Comte Riant and of most of his collaborators has left much to be done.

The sources of the Crusades are almost inexhaustible, and though we have tried to furnish the student with ample bibliographical notices, we can hardly claim completeness. Since most nations of medieval Europe became involved to varying degrees in this widespread movement, it becomes incumbent on the historian of the Crusade to search for his material in the archives of all these nations and in all their languages. For example, the publications of the Palestine Exploration Fund ** and the Deutsche Palaestina-Verein; the *Bibliotheca Geographorum Arabicorum;* † the three *Patrologias* (*Latina, Graeca,* and *Orientalis*) ; the *Acta Sanctorum* and *Acta Bollandiana;* the

* See below, Monumental Collections, section III.
** See below, Monumental Collections, section II.
† See below, Monumental Collections, section VII.

monumental national collections of chronicles (such as the *Rolls Series* and the *Monumenta Germaniae Historica*); and the numerous collections of French history. These and all manner of other source material must be combed by the serious student. The *Regesta Pontificum Romanorum,* the archives of the Military Orders of Religion, and the Venetian and Genoese archive material are vital too; and older publications, such as the *Rerum Italicarum Scriptores* (ed. Muratori, and more recently Carducci), Rymer's *Foedera,* and Raynaldi's *Annales Ecclesiastici* cannot be overlooked. An attempt is made to bring these remarks up to date in the General Bibliography.

The Arabic sources present a greater problem. The Arabic materials in the *Recueil,* accompanied by translations into French, though of great service, have lagged behind the canons of modern research. They are extracts, and thus defective in principle. The extracts are given without reference to their place in the original manuscript. Further, the translations are often free and unreliable. The whole position with regard to the Oriental sources available in European languages is lamentable, and the serious student is advised to go to the original texts for the exact words of each chronicler. Masses of original material have seen the light since the days of the *Recueil.* The writings of ibn al-Athīr, ibn Wāṣil, ibn al-Furāt, ibn Taghri Bardi, al-Maqrīzi and others now available in print must be consulted, preferably in their original form.

How can we achieve this? Sir Hamilton Gibb declared at the 1955 convention of the American Historical Association that by the time the Orientalist has finished his philological inquiry into Arabic sources, he has little time or energy left for the use of the documents to serve historical writing. Yet it is a tragedy that the original texts cannot be used to their full value by the historian of the Crusade. The writers of the standard reference works on the Cru-

sades, including Röhricht, Grousset, and Runciman, have
had no direct access to the Arabic sources, and their knowledge of the Islamic point of view is limited to a few extracts
rendered into a European language. As we step out of the
early Crusades into the area of the later movement, we find
that only a small fraction of the available material is extant in any form other than the original Arabic.

May we assume that the authoritative and definitive history of the Crusade is still to be written? Painstaking efforts
have been exerted to meet this need by marshaling an international body of historians and Orientalists to collabo-
rate in the Pennsylvania *History of the Crusades* in five
monumental volumes.* The spirit of the late Professor
John L. LaMonte lives in the project, which will supersede
everything that has hitherto appeared on the subject. The
services it will render to scholars are immeasurable. Nevertheless, it will no doubt suffer from the shortcomings in-
herent in all collective writing on so wide a scale. We can
already detect oversight in regard to the history of the
Counter-Crusade as a separate entity worthy of special attention.

The real need in the field of the Crusades is for mono-
graphs by specialists, scores of them, on biographies of
leading Crusaders, given events, a source—Western or
Oriental—, a travel relation, a propagandist text, a castle
or a monument, numismatic evidence, sigillography, epig-
raphy, and a whole host of other possibilities. These are the
rocks on which the general historian of the Crusade can
build his edifice. Until the present, historians have built
and are still indefatigably building on somewhat sandy
soil.

Crusade historiography is a subject for a comprehensive
monograph as yet unwritten. Here is a short bibliography

* Two volumes have been published, by M. W. Baldwin and R. L.
Wolff; see below, General Bibliography, section IV. 1, for citations.

which may be utilized for the fulfillment of a considerable task. For the Western side of the picture, the following works merit consultation.

Boase, T. S. R.: "Recent Developments in Crusading Historiography," *History*, N.S., XXII–1937, 110–25.

Boehn, L.: "Die Gesta Tancredi des Ranulf von Caen, Ein Beitrag zur Geschichtsschreibung der Normannen um 1100," *Historisches Jahrbuch*, LXXV–1956, 47–72.

Bourgin, G.: *Guibert de Nogent, Histoire de sa vie (Collection des textes pour servir à l'étude et à l'enseignement de l'histoire)*, Paris 1907.

Bovée, D.: *The Sources of the Third Crusade* (Dissert.), University of Minnesota, Minneapolis, Minn., 1938.

Buckler, G.: *Anna Comnena*, Oxford 1929.

Cutolo, A.: "Bibliografia critica delle fonti narrative della Prima Crociata," *Bullettino dell' Istituto Storico italiano per il Medio Evo e Archivio Muratoriano*, L–1944, 1–30.

Déherain, H.: "Les Origines du *Recueil des Historiens des Croisades*," *J.S.* 1919 (Sept.–Oct.), 260–66.

Duparc-Quioc, S.: "La Conquête de Jérusalem—Le Cycle de la Croisade," *Hautes Études*, 1955—fasc. 305.

Funk, P.: *Jacob von Vitry, Leben und Werke*, Leipzig 1909.

Glaesner, H.: "La Prise d'Antioche en 1098 dans la littérature épique française," *Rev. Belge*, XIX–1940, 65–85.

———: "Raoul de Caen, historien et écrivain," *Rev. Écc.*, XLVI–1951, 1–21.

Grégoire, H.: "Notes sur Anne Comnène," *Byzantion*, III–1926, 311–17.

Gutsch, M. R.: "A Twelfth Century Preacher—Fulk of Neuilly," in Paetow, *The Crusades and Other Historical Essays Presented to Dana C. Munro*, N.Y. 1928, 183–206.

Jorga, N.: *Les Narrateurs de la Première Croisade*, Paris 1928.

Klimke, C.: *Die Quellen zur Geschichte des vierten Kreuzzuges*, Breslau 1875.

Krey, A. C.: *The First Crusade: The Account of Eye-witnesses and Participants*, Gloucester, Mass., 1958; reproduction of original edition by Princeton University Press, 1921.

————: "William of Tyre—the Making of an Historian in the Middle Ages," *Speculum*, XVI–1941, 149–66.

Kugler, B.: *Albert von Aachen*, Stuttgart 1885.

LaMonte, J. L.: "The Significance of the Crusaders' States in Medieval History," *Byzantion*, XV–1940–41, 300–15.

————: "Some Problems of Crusading Historiography," *Speculum*, XV–1940, 57–75.

Munro, D. C.: "A Crusader—Foucher de Chartres," *Speculum*, VII–1932, 321–35.

Neumann, C.: *Griechische Geschichtsschreiber und Geschichtsquellen im 12. Jahrhundert—Studien zu Anna Comnena, Theod. Prodromus, Joh. Cinnamus*, Leipzig 1888.

Palumbo, P. E.: "Quadro Storico delle Crociate," *Archivio della Deputazione romana di Storia Patria*, LXIII–1945, 1–31.

Sánchez Alonso, B.: *Historia de la historiografía española*, 3 vols., Madrid 1941–50. (Especially helpful on the Reconquista.)

Sybel, H. von: *The History and Literature of the Crusades*, ed. and trans. by Lady Duff Gordon, London 1861; reprinted by Routledge, n.d.

Thatcher, P. J.: "Latin Sources of the First Crusade," *Annual Report of the American Historical Association*, I–1900, 499–509.

Thurot, Ch.: "Études critiques sur les historiens des croisades," *R.H.* I–1876; pt. 1: "De l'ouvrage anonyme intitulé Gesta Francorum et aliorum Hierosolymitanorum," 67–77; pt. 2: "Baudri de Bourgueil," 372–86.

Vasiliev, A.: "The Study of Byzantine History," in *History of the Byzantine Empire,* in 1 vol., Madison, Wisc., 1952, 3–42.

Verlet-Reaubourg, N.: "L'Ocuvre de Richart le Pèlerin et de Graindor de Douai, connue sous le nom de Chanson d'Antioche," *E. de C.*, Paris 1932, 153–58.

Witzel, H. J.: "Le Problème de l'auteur des Gesta Francorum et aliorum Hierosolymitanorum," *Le Moyen Âge*, LXI–1955, 319–28.

S. Runciman has devoted a special appendix in each volume of his work to a survey of the principal sources of the various periods of the Crusade, classifying them as

Greek, Latin, Arabic, Armenian, Syriac, Georgian, and Slavonic. His statements are useful on European sources but inadequate on Oriental materials. See Runciman: *A History of the Crusades,* 3 vols., Cambridge 1951–54; Vol. I (327 ff), Vol. II (475 ff), and Vol. III (481 ff).

For the Greek literature consult Krumbacher and Muralt (see below, General Bibliography, section II.2).

For the Arabic side of the picture, useful gleanings may be reaped from the notes compiled by Reinaud in a special volume: *Chroniques Arabes,* Paris 1829, and from Michaud's *Bibliothèque,* as well as from the introductory and supplementary notes to the volumes of the Historiens Orientaux in the *Recueil des Historiens des Croisades.**

Although Arabic historiography is still in its infancy, a number of independent studies on some of its aspects are extant and listed below. These, however, must be tied up with the general framework of Arabic thought.** Most of the medieval historians of the Arabs were diversified in their knowledge and authorship, men who tried their hand at more than one branch of the humanities, and it is therefore necessary for a researcher in one domain to follow his subject into distant disciplines. The more relevant works on the historians are:

'Ammār, 'Abbās: *Ibn Khaldoun's Prolegomena to History* (Dissert.), Cambridge 1941.
'Ayad, M. Kāmil: "Die Anfang der arabischen Geschichtsschreibung," *Geist und Gessellschaft, K. Breysig zu seinem sechzigste geburtstage,* 3 vols. in 1, III, Breslau [1927–28], 35–48.
Cahen, C.: *La Syrie du Nord à l'Époque des Croisades,* Paris 1940, 33 ff.
Gabrieli, F.: "Gli Ospitalieri di San Giovanni negli storici musulmani delle Crociate," *Annuario della R. Scuola Archeologica di Atene,* VIII–IX–1929, 345–56.

* For the *Recueil* and the *Bibliothèque,* see below, Monumental Collections, sections I and V.
** See Atiya: *Crusade, Commerce and Culture,* ch. 6.

————: *Storici Arabi delle Crociate* (*Scrittori di Storia*, no. 6), Rome 1957.

Gibb, H.A.R.: "The Arabic Sources for the Life of Saladin," *Speculum*, XXV–1950, 58–72.

————: "Notes on the Arabic Materials for the History of the Early Crusades," *Bulletin of the School of Oriental Studies*, VII–1935, 739–54.

————: "Ta'rīkh," in the *Encyclopaedia of Islam*, Supp. V, Leiden 1938, 233–45.

Gumplowicz, L.: *Ibn Chaldun, ein arabischer Soziologie des 14. Jahrhunderts*, Innsbruck 1890.

al-Ḥusari, Sāṭi: *Dirāsat 'an Muqaddimat ibn Khaldūn* (Studies in ibn Khaldūn's "Prologomena"), Cairo and Bagdad 1961.

Ḥussein, Taha: *Étude analytique et critique de la philosophie sociale d'Ibn Khaldoun*, Paris 1917.

'Inān, Muḥammad 'Abdallah: *Ibn Khaldūn, His Life and Work*, English trans. from Arabic, Lahore 1941.

Issawi, C. (trans.): *An Arab Philosophy of History, Selections from the Prolegomena of Ibn Khaldūn of Tunis (1332–1406)*, London 1950.

Khaldūn, ibn (d. 1406): "Muqaddimah," French trans. by W. M. de Slane, *Notices et extraits des Mss. de la Bibliothèque Impériale*, XIX–XXI, Paris 1863–68; English trans. by F. Rosenthal, published by the Bollingen Foundation, 3 vols., N.Y. 1958 (does not supersede the earlier French trans. in quality). (This is the famous "Prolegomena" to the "Universal History," which represents the height of Arabic philosophy of history and the birth of systematic study of sociology in the Middle Ages. Original texts of the "Prolegomena" and the "History" are extant in various editions, of which the better known ones appeared in Paris in 1858, by E. Quatremère, and in Cairo, 1867 ff.)

Kratchkovsky, I. Y.: *Among Arabic Manuscripts—Memories of Libraries and Men*, trans. by Tatiana Minorsky, Leiden 1953.

Lewis, B.: "The Sources of the History of the Syrian Assassins," *Speculum*, XXVII–1952, 475–89.

Mahdi, M.: *Ibn Khaldūn's Philosophy of History*, London 1957. (See 147 ff, on ibn Khaldūn's "Dialectical Study of Islamic Historiography." Cf. also ibn Khaldūn: "Muqaddimah," above.)

Margoliouth, D. S.: *Lectures on Arabic Historians*, Calcutta 1930.

Richter, G.: "Medieval Arabic Historiography," trans. and ed. by M. Saber Khan, *I.C.*, XXXIII–1959–no. 4, 240 ff, and XXXIV–1960–no. 2, 139 ff.

Rosenthal, F.: *A History of Muslim Historiography*, Leiden 1952.

al-Sakhāwi, Shams al-Dīn Muḥammad ibn ʿAbd al-Rahmān (d. 1496): *Al-I ʿlān bil-Taubīkh li-man dhamma al-Taʾ rīkh* (History of Arab Historians), Damascus 1930.

Sinor, Denis: *Orientalism and History*, Cambridge 1954.

Wüstenfeld, F.: *Die Geschichtsschreiber der Araber und ihre Werke*, Göttingen 1882.

The bibliographical works of Brockelmann, Graf, Spuler and Forrer, Hajji Khalifah, etc. (see below, General Bibliography, section I.1 and section I.2) are equally indispensable for any study of Arabic historiography. Histories of Arabic literature, too—*e.g.*, by Nicholson, Gibb, Huart, Abd al-Jalil, etc.—contain useful gleanings on the subject (see below, General Bibliography, section IV.7, Literature).

Monumental Collections

I. RECUEIL DES HISTORIENS DES CROISADES

Rapporteurs: Hase, Quatremère, Reinaud, Guérard, Beugnot
Paris, 1841–1906

A. Historiens Occidentaux
5 vols., 1844–95.

Tome I in 2 parts (Paris 1844) : Latin chronicle of William of Tyre (Guillaume de Tyr or Ṣūr), written in the second half of the 12th century to the year 1184 A.D., entitled "Historia rerum in partibus transmarinis gestarum a tempore successorum Mahumeth usque ad annum Domini MCLXXXIV," with a Middle French translation entitled "L'estoire de Éracles empéreur et la conqueste de la Terre d'outremer."

Tome II (Paris 1859) : French continuations of William of Tyre, first to 1229, then from 1229 to 1261 A.D. Followed by analytical chronological table of contents of both chronicle and continuations. 642 ff.

Tome III (Paris 1866) : Latin chronicles of the First Crusade, ten in number, listed as follows:

1–3. Petri Tudebodi seu Tudebovis:
    a. Historia de Hierosolymitane Itinere. 1 ff.
    b. Gesta francorum et aliorum Hierosolymitanorum seu Tudebodus abbreviatus. 119 ff.
    c. Tudebodus imitatus et continuatus. Historia peregrinorum euntium Jeruselymam ad Liberandum Sanctum Sepulcrum de potestate ethnicorum. 165 ff.
4. Raimundi de Aguilers canonici Podiensis Historia francorum qui ceperunt Iherusalem. 231 ff.
5. Historia Iherosolymitana Gesta Francorum Iherusalem peregrinantium ab anno Domini MCXV usque ad annum MCXXVII, Auctore domno Fulcherio Carnotensi. 310 ff.
6. Gesta Francorum expugnantium Iherusalem. 487 ff.
7. Secunda Pars Historiae Iherosolimitanae. 545 ff.
8. Gesta Tancredi in expeditione Hierosolymitana, Auctore Radulfo Cadomensi ejus familiari. 587 ff.
9. Roberti monachi Historia Iherosolimitana. 717 ff.
10. Stephani, comitis Carnotensis atque Anselmi de Ribodi Monte Epistolae. 883 ff.

Tome IV (Paris 1879) : More Latin chronicles of the First Crusade—Baudri de Dol, Guibert de Nogent, and Albert d'Aix.

1. Baldrici episcopi Dolensis Historia Jherosolimitana. 1 ff.
2. Historia quae dicitur Gesta Dei per Francos edita a venerabili domno Guiberto, abbati monasterii Sanctae Mariae Novigenti. 113 ff.
3. Alberti Aquensis Historia Hierosolymitana. 265 ff.

Tome V (Paris 1895) : Some major and some minor chronicles including Ekkehard, Caffaro, Gautier le chancelier, the Anonymous History of the First Crusade, and others listed below.

1. Ekkehardi abbatis Uraugiensis, Hierosolymita. 11 ff.
2. Cafari de Caschifelone, Genuensis consulis, De liberatione civitatum Orientis. 41 ff.

3. Galterii, cancellarii Antiocheni, Bella Antiochena, 1114–1119 A.D.   75 ff.

4. Balduini III, Historia Nicaeana vel Antiochena.   133 ff.

5. Theodori Palidensis, Narratio profectionis Godefridi ducis ad Jerusalem.   187 ff.

6. Passiones Beati Theimonis.   199 ff.

7. Documenta Lipsanographica ad I. bellum sacrum spectantia. (Eleven minor tracts on the First Crusade.)   225 ff.

8. Primi belli sacri narrationes minores. (Fourteen minor tracts on the First Crusade.)   341 ff.

9. Exordium Hospitalariorum. (Six tracts on Hospitallers.)   339 ff.

10. Anonymi Rhenani Historia et gesta Gotfridi, historia de obsidione Terrae Sanctae anno MXCVI.   437 ff.

11. Benedicti de Accoltis, aretini, Historia Gotefridi.   525 ff.

12. Li estoire de Jerusalem et d'Antioche.   621 ff.

13. Itinerario di la gran militia a la Pavese.   649 ff.

14. Fulco—Historia gestarum viae nostri temporis Jerosolymitanae. (Poem.)   693 ff.

15. Gilo—Historia Gilonis cardinalis episcopi de via Hierosolymitana. (Another poem.)   725 ff.

ADDITIONAL NOTES

1. For William of Tyre, see M. Solloch's edition of the Latin continuation, Leipzig 1934; Paulin Paris's edition of 13th-century French trans.: *Guillaume de Tyr et ses Continuateurs*, 2 vols., Paris 1879–80; and English trans. by E. A. Babcock and A. C. Krey: *A History of Deeds Beyond the Sea (Records)*, 2 vols., N.Y. 1943 (see below, section VI). William of Tyre's work attracted attention from the earliest days of printing. Among his early translators was William Caxton: *Godefroy of Bologne or the Siege and Conquest of Jerusalem,* 1481; later re-edited by M. N. Colvin for the Early English Text Society, London 1893. A French edition by G. de Préau appeared in Paris in 1573, and an Italian version by M. G. Horologgi appeared in Venice in 1562.

2. Other editions of the anonymous chronicle ascribed to Tudebodus may be found in L. Bréhier: *Histoire anonyme de la Première Croisade,* Paris 1924; in H. Hagenmeyer (ed.):

Anonymi gesta Francorum Hierosolimitanorum, Heidelberg 1890; and in B. Lees (ed.) : *Anonymi gesta Francorum Hierosolimitanorum,* Oxford 1924.

3. For Fulcher of Chartres, see H. Hagenmeyer (ed.) : *Gesta Francorum* . . . , Heidelberg 1913; and English trans. by M. E. McGinty: *Chronicle of the First Crusade,* Philadelphia 1941.

4. For Ekkehard, see H. Hagenmeyer (ed.) : *Hierosolymita,* Tübingen 1877.

5. For Cafari de Caschifelone, see L. T. Belgrano and C. Imperiale di Santangelo: *Annali genovesi di Caffaro e dei suoi continuatori (Fonti per la Storia d'Italia)* , 5 vols., Rome and Genoa 1890–1929; and Italian trans. by C. Roccatagliata-Ceccardi and G. Monleone, 9 vols., Genoa 1924–30.

6. Other Western sources for the First Crusade include:

Epistolae et chartae ad historiam primi belli sacri spectantes quae supersunt aevo aequales, published as *Die Kreuzzugsbriefe aus den Jahren 1088–1100, Ein Quellensammlung zur Geschichte des Erstenkreuzzüges,* Innsbruck 1901.

Hagenmeyer, H.: *Die Kreuzzugsbriefe aus den Jahren 1088–1100,* Innsbruck 1902.

Hippeau, Ch. (ed.) : *La Conquête de Jerusalem,* Paris 1868.

Krey, A. C.: *The First Crusade: The Accounts of Eye-Witnesses and Participants,* Gloucester, Mass., 1958; reproduction of original edition by Princeton University Press, 1921, containing extracts in English from sources.

Le Prévost (ed.) : *Orderici Vitali Angligenae Historiae ecclesiasticae libri XIII ex veteris codicis Uticensis collectione,* 4 vols., Paris 1838–40.

Meyer, P.: "Un récit en vers français de la Première Croisade fondé sur Baudri de Bourgueil," *Romania,* V–1876, 1–63, and VI–1877, 489–94.

Paris, P. (ed.) : *La Chanson d'Antioche,* 2 vols., Paris 1848.
———: *Chanson du Chevalier au Cygne;* French ed. by Hippeau, 2 vols., Paris 1874–77; Flemish ed. by Reiffenberg and Borgnet, 3 vols., Brussels 1846–59.

7. Also see General Bibliography, below, section IV. 1.

B. Lois

2 vols., 1841–43. Assises de Jérusalem ou Recueil des ouvrages de jurisprudence composés pendant le XIIIᵉ siècle dans les Royaumes de Jérusalem et de Chypre.

Tome I (Paris 1841) : Assises de le Haute Cour, ed. M. le Comte Beugnot, with introduction (i–lxxxvii), and including the following texts:

1. Livre de Jean d'Ibelin. (By far the fullest and most elaborate work of jurisprudence of its kind for the period.)   1 ff.
2. Livre de Geoffroy le Tort.   433 ff.
3. Livre de Jacques d'Ibelin.   451 ff.
4. Livre de Philippe de Navarre.   469 ff.
5. La Clef des Assises de la Haute Cour du royaume de Jérusalem et de Chypre.   573 ff.
6. Le Livre au Roy.   601 ff.

Tome II (Paris 1843) : Assises de la Cour des Bourgeois, ed. M. le Comte Beugnot, with introduction (i–lxxiv), and including the following texts:

1. Livre des Assises de la Cour des Bourgeois.   3 ff.
2. Abrégé du Livre des Assises de la Cour des Bourgeois.   277 ff.
3. Bans et Ordonnances des rois de Chypre.   353 ff.
4. Formules. (Essential for the student of medieval diplomatics.)   381 ff.

These books are followed by a special "Appendice" containing a series of documents of the highest importance for the constitutional, military, and political structure of the Latin kingdoms in the East.

1. Documents relatifs à la successibilité au trône et à la régence.   393 ff.
2. Document relatif au service militaire.   423 ff.
3. Les Lignages d'Outremer.   441 ff.
4. Chartes. (Contains 52 charters dated from 1103 to 1211 A.D., plus two charters undated but apparently issued in or after 1240 A.D.)   475 ff.

ADDITIONAL NOTES

Further material and studies on the Assizes may be found in the following works:

Alishinian, G.: *Les Assises d'Antioche* (Armenian text and French trans.), Venice 1876.

Grandclaude, M.: *Étude Critique sur les Livres des Assises de Jérusalem*, Paris 1932.

Hayak, D.: *Le Droit franc en Syrie pendant les croisades*, Paris 1925.

Monnier, F.: *Godefroi de Bouillon et les Assises de Jerusalem*, Paris 1874.

Prawer, J.: "The 'Assise de Tenure' and the 'Assise de Vente,'—A Study of Landed Property in the Latin Kingdom," *Economic History Review*, 2nd ser., IV–1951, 77–88.

———: "L'Établissement des coutumes de marché à Saint-Jean d'Acre et la date de composition du 'Livre des Assises des Bourgeois'," *Revue Historique de Droit Français et Étranger*, 1951, 329–51.

———: "Étude préliminaire sur les sources de la composition du 'Livre des Assises des Bourgeois,'" *Revue Historique de Droit Français et Étranger*, 1954, 198–227, 358–82.

Recoura, G. (ed.): *Les Assises de Romanie*, Paris 1930.

Rozière, E. de: *Cartulaire de l'Église de Saint-Sépulcre*, Paris 1849.

Topping, P. W.: *Feudal Institutions as Revealed in the Assizes of Romania, the Law Code of Frankish Greece*, Philadelphia 1949. (Translation of texts with commentary.)

———: "The Formation of the Assizes of Romanie," *Byzantion*, XVII–1944–45, 304–14.

C. Historiens Orientaux
5 vols., 1872–1906.

Work on the Arabic sources was begun by Georges-François Berthereau for the *Histoire de la Congrégation de Saint-Maur* around the middle of the eighteenth century. This was interrupted by the fall of the monarchy in France, until a commission of the "Institut" in 1801 appointed Silvestre de Sacy to examine the notes and manuscripts of Dom Berthereau. He did this and submitted a list of their contents. In 1813 the documents were acquired by the Bibliothèque Nationale in Paris. Afterwards, Reinaud resumed the publication of his volume entitled *Extraits des historiens arabes relatifs aux guerres des croisades.* In 1834 the Académie decided to publish the Arabic historians separately and named Reinaud and Quatremère for the joint project. Started in 1837, the work was again suspended, to be resumed in 1850 by Reinaud in collaboration with Defréméry. After preparing the material for an introduction, Defréméry died and was succeeded by de Slane, who completely revised the French version of Abu-l-Fidā. De Slane died while working on the third volume, which was completed by Barbier de Meynard.

It is unfortunate that the published text throughout the whole series represents extracts which the editors deemed relevant, while the rest was dropped without indication as to where the gaps were located or how long they might be. The French is to be considered merely as a version to bring out the meaning of the original rather than as an accurate and literal translation.

Tome I (Paris 1872). Ed. Reinaud, later de Slane.

1. Introduction (i–lxxi) by de Slane. (Contains useful notes on the dynasties of the period, chronological tables, and remarks on some Arab historians, as well as the manuscripts employed and the technique followed in the preparation of the texts.)
2. Resumé de l'Histoire des Croisades, tiré des Annales d'aboû'l Feda. ("Al-Mukhtaṣar fi Akhbār al-Bashar," by Abu-l-Fidā Ismāʿīl, ruler of Hamah. Text beginning with year 485 A.H./1092–93 A.D. and ending with year 702 A.H./1302–03 A.D.) 1–165.
3. Autobiographie d'Aboû'l-Feda. (In French only.) 168–80.
4. Extrait de la Chronique intitulée Kamel-Altevarykh par Ibn-Alatyr. ("Kitāb al-Kāmil fi al-Tārīkh," by ibn al-Athīr, d. 1223 A.D. Extract from the year 491 A.H./1098 A.D. to 585 A.H./1189–90 A.D.) 189–744.
5. Appendice (745–56) by de Slane. (Contains additional material on the lives of Abu-l-Fidā' and ibn al-Athīr, as well as as their works.)

Tome II, Part I (Paris 1887). Ed. M. de Slane and Barbier de Meynard.

Extrait de la Chronique intitulée Kamel-Altevarykh par Ibn-Alatyr. (Continuation of Tome I from the year 585 A.H./1189–90 A.D. to 673 A.H./1274–75 A.D.) 3–250.

Tome II, Part II (Paris 1876). Ed. M. de Slane and Barbier de Meynard.

Histoire des Atabecs de Mosul par Ibn al-Athīr. ("Tārīkh al-Daulah al-Atābikiyah, Mulūk al-Mauṣil," by ibn al-Athīr. Begins with the reign of Aq-Sonqor in 477 A.H./1084–85 A.D. and ends in the reign of al-Malik al-Qāhir Masʿūd II, 607 A.H./1211 A.D.) 5–375.

Tome III (Paris 1884). This volume is devoted to the Arabic sources dealing with the life of Saladin.

1. Anecdotes et Beaux traits de la Vie du Sultan Youssof (Ṣalâh ed-Dîn). ("Al-Nawādir al-Sulṭāniyah wa-l-Maḥāsin al-Yūsufiyah," by Bahāʾ-al-Din Yūsuf ibn Rāfiʿ ibn Tamīm, known as ibn Shaddād, judge of Aleppo, d. 1234 A.D., beginning with the birth of Saladin and concluding with the year 589 A.H./1193 A.D.) 3–370.

2. Notice sur Bha ed-Din Aboul-Mehacen ibn Cheddad, extraite du Dictionnaire biographique d'ibn Kallican. (This biography is extracted from ibn Khallikān's "Kitāb Wafiyāt al-Aʿyan," with some "Observations complémentaires.") 379–93, 395–96.

3. Extraits de la vie du sultan Salah ed-Din d'ibn Khallican. 401–30.

4. Extrait de l'Autobiographie d'Abd el-Latif. ("Sīrat Muwaffaq-al-Dīn ʿAbd-al-Laṭīf al-Baghdādi," d. 1231 A.D.) 437–39.

5. Extrait du voyage d'ibn Djobeir. ("Riḥlah," by ibn Jubayr, d. 1217 A.D.) 445–56.

6. Extraits d'ibn Moyesses. ("Taʾrīkh," by ibn Muyassir, who wrote between 676 A.H./1277 A.D. and 690 A.H./1291 A.D.) 461–73.

7. Extraits du Nodjoum ez-Zahireh, par Abou'l-Mehacen. 481–509.

8. Extraits du Mirat ez-Zeman. ("Mirʾat al-Zamān fī Taʾrīkh

al-Aiyām, by Sibṭ ibn al-Jauzi, d. 654 A.H./1256 A.D.) 517–70.

9. Extraits de la Chronique d'Alep par Kemal ed-Din. ("Ta'rī<u>kh</u> Halab," by Kamāl-al-Dīn, known as Abu Ḥāfiẓ and ibn al-'Adīm, d. 660 A.H./1262 A.D., prefaced by Barbier de Meynard.) 578–690.

10. Extraits du Dictionnaire biographique de Kemal ed-Din. ("Bug<u>h</u>yat al-Ṭalab fī Ta'rī<u>kh</u> Ḥalab," containing lives of Ismā'īl ibn Būri, al-malik al-ṣāliḥ Ismā'īl ibn Nūr-al-Dīn, Aq-Sunqur and Alp Arslān, son of Riḍwān.) 696–732.

Tome IV (Paris 1898). Ed. A. C. Barbier de Meynard.

"Le Livre des deux jardins"; Histoire des deux règnes, celui de Nour ed-Din et celui de Salah ed-Din. (Extracts from "Kitāb al-Rauḍatain fī A<u>kh</u>bār al-Daulatain al-Nūriyah wa-l-Ṣalāhiyah," by Abu Shāmah, d. 1267 A.D., covering the period from 541 A.H./1146–47 A.D., year of Zangi's death, to 586 A.H./1190–91 A.D., year of the fall of Acre to the Franks. Abu Shāmah witnessed most of the events of the Second and Third Crusades, the weakening of the kingdom of Jerusalem leading to the monstrous defeat of Hittin, and the capitulation of Jerusalem in 1187 A.D.) 3–522.

Tome V (Paris 1906). Continued from Tome IV.

1. "Le Livre des deux jardins"; Histoire des deux règnes, celui de Nour ed-Din et celui de Salah ed-Din. (By the same author, Abu Shāmah, covering the years 587 A.H./1191–92 A.D. to 665 A.H./1266–67 A.D.) 3–206.

2. Autobiographie d'Abou Chamah, tirée du Complément (Dzeil) du "Livre des deux jardins." (Text and translation in French of this interesting autobiography, wherein the writer gives his full name as 'Abd-al-Rahmān ibn Ismā'īl ibn Ibrāhīm ibn 'U<u>th</u>mān ibn Abi-Bakr ibn Ibrāhīm ibn Muḥammad al-Maqdisi, known as Abu Shāmah. He speaks of his pilgrimages, his personal relationships, lists his works, and provides excerpts from his poetry.) 207–16.

ADDITIONAL NOTES

1. Detailed analytical bibliographies of Arabic sources on the Crusade are to be found in C. Cahen: *La Syrie du Nord à*

l'Époque des Croisades, Paris 1940; and in Atiya: *The Crusade in the Later Middle Ages,* London 1938.

2. The following works and textual editions should also be consulted as requisite supplementation to this part of the *Recueil:*

Abu'-l-fidā': *Al-Mukhtaṣar,* 4 vols., Istanbul 1286 A.H./1869–70 A.D.

Abu-l-Mahāsin: *Al-Nujum,* 9 vols., Cairo 1929–47. (Older edition in the *University of California Publications in Semitic Philology,* by W. Popper, is equally useful.)

Abu-Shāmah: *Al-Rawḍatain,* 2 vols., Cairo 1287–88 A.H./1870–71 A.D.; and *Dhail* (Supp.), Cairo 1947. (New ed. of Abu-Shāmah, from a Copenhagen MS., is in progress, by Ḥilmy Aḥmad, in Cairo.)

al-Athīr, ibn: "Kitāb al-Kāmil fi al-Ta'rīkh" (Universal History), ed. by C. J. Tornberg, *Chronicon quod perfectissimum inscribitur,* 14 vols., Leiden 1851–76.

Blochet, E.: "Histoire d'Alep de Kamāl-al-Dīn; version française d'après le texte arabe," *Rev. Or. Lat.,* III–1895, 509–65; IV–1896, 145–225; V–1897, 37–107; VI–1898, 1–49.

————: "Histoire d'Égypte de Makrizi, traduction française accompagnée de notes géographiques et historiques," *Rev. Or. Lat.,* VI–1898, 435–89; VIII–1900–01, 165–212, 501–53; IX–1902, 6–163, 466–530; X–1903–04; XI–1905–08, 192–239 (followed by "Extraits de l'Histoire des Patriarches d'Alexandrie relatifs au siège de Damiette sous le règne d'al-Malik al-Kamil," 240–60). (This is the famous "Kitāb al-Sulūk." Cf. editions by Quatremère and Ziada, below.)

Cahen, C.: "La Chronique abrégée d'al-Azimi," *J.A.,* 1938, 353–448.

————: "Une Chronique Syrienne du VIe–XIIe siècles," *Bulletin d'Études Orientales,* VII–VIII–1937–38, 113–58.

Derenbourg, H.: "Autobiographie d'Ousama; traduction française d'après le texte arabe," *Rev. Or. Lat.,* II–1894, 327–565; followed by appendix containing extracts from the Arab historians al-Dhahabi, ibn al-Athīr, and Abu Shāmah, as well as index of proper names.

Gabrieli, F.: *Storici Arabi delle Crociate,* Turin 1957. (Italian trans. of selections from Arabic chroniclers.)

Imad ad-Din: *Conquête de la Syrie et de la Palestine par Salah ed-Din*, ed. and French trans. by C. de Landberg, Leiden 1888.

al-Jauzi, Sibṭ ibn: *Mir'at al-Zamān*, ed. by J. R. Jewett, Chicago 1907.

Khaldūn, ibn: "Muqaddimah," French trans. by W. M. de Slane, in *Notices et Extraits des* MSS. *de la Bibliothèque Impériale*, XIX–XXI, Paris 1863–68.

Munqidh, 'Usāmah ibn (d. 1188): *An Arab-Syrian Gentleman and Warrior in the Period of the Crusades: Memoirs of Usamah ibn-Munqidh*, trans. from Arabic MS by P. K. Hitti (*Records*), N.Y. 1929 (see below, section VI) ; also ed. by G. R. Potter, N.Y. 1929.

Nāṣirī-Khusrau: *Sefar-Nameh*, in Arabic from the Persian original MS., prepared by Yaḥyā al-Khashshāb, Cairo 1945. (The old English rendering by Guy Le Strange: *Diary of a Journey through Syria and Palestine*, London 1887, is still useful.)

al-Qalānisī, ibn (d. 1140): *Khail Ta'rīsh Dimashq, a contination of the Damascene Chronicle of the Crusades*, Arabic ed. by H. F. Amedroz, Leiden 1908; selections in English by H. A. R. Gibb: *The Damascus Chronicle of the Crusades*, London 1932.

Quatremère, F.: *Histoire des Sultans Mamelouks*, 2 vols., Paris 1837–45. (This is part of Maqrizi's chronicle entitled "Kitāb al-Sulūk," ed. in progress by M. M. Ziada, Cairo 1934 ff.)

Sacy, S. de: ibn al-'Adīm (1095–1173 A.D.) , "Extraits de l'Histoire d'Alep," in Röhricht: *Beiträge zur Geschichte des Kreuzzüge*, I, Berlin 1874–78, 209–346; for the years 1146–1242, see French trans. by E. Blochet: "Histoire d'Alep," *Rev. Or. Lat.*, IV–VI– 1896–98–1900 (abridged and inaccurate) .

Serverus, bishop of Ashmunein: "History of the Patriarchs of the Coptic Church of Alexandria," Arabic text and English trans. by B. Evetts, in *Patr. Or.*, 4 fasc., Paris 1907 ff; continued for the Society of Coptic Archaeology by A. S. Atiya, O. H. E. Burmester, and Y. Abd-al-Massih, in 4 fasc., Cairo 1948–59.

Wāsil, ibn: "Chronicle" of the Aiyubid period, now being edited by G. Shayal, to be published by the Ministry of Education, Cairo.

Zurayk, C. K. (ed.) : *The History of ibn al-Furāt*, 9 vols., Beirut 1936–38.

D. Historiens Grecs

2 vols., 1875–81. Hase, Alexandre, and E. M. (Prefaces for both volumes are signed E.M.)

Tome I (Paris 1875)

Preface (i–xvii). Scriptores Graeci bellorum a Francis Dei signa sequentibus in Syria susceptorum.

1. Pars Prima: De rebus proxime ante primam nostrorum expeditionem Asiaticam inter Asiaticam inter Graecos Turcasque gestis. A.D. 1068–1096. (Includes chronicles of Michael Attaliata and Michael Psellus; Greek excerpts and Latin translation.) 3–99. Notes, 101–54.
2. Pars Secunda: De prima expeditione occidentalium ad sacra loca recuperanda. 1096–1118. (Excerpts from Anna Comnena in Greek, with translation in Latin.) 4–203.
3. Pars Tertia: De secunda tertiaque expeditionibus. Transitio, 1096, 1096–1118, 1118–1137 A.D. (John Cinnamus and Nicetas Choniates, covering the period 1137–1190.) 207–337.
4. Pars Quarta: Nicetas Choniates, 1191–1206 A.D. (Excerpts in Greek with Latin translation. Nicetas was an eyewitness of events of his time.) 341–514.
5. Pars Quinta. Excerpta Minora:
   a. Ex Joannis Zonarae Annalium, 1096–1099 A.D. 517–18.
   b. Ex Michaelis Glycae Annalium, 1096–1104 A.D. 518.
   c. Ex Nicephori Gregorae Historiarum Byzantinarum, 1096–1099 A.D. 519 ff.
   d. Ex Ephraemio Chronographo, 1096–1108 A.D. 523 ff.
   e. Joannes Phocas, 1177 A.D. (Native of Crete, monk of Patmos, Phocas fought in the armies of Manuel Palaeologus.) 527–58.
   f. Neophytus Presbyter, 1191 A.D. (Neophytus was a native of Cyprus.) 559–63.
   g. Ex Georgio Acropolita, 1183–1206. 563–80.
   h. Ex Libro de Syria expugnata, 1096–1204 A.D. (Poem.) 581–623.
   i. Ex Phraemio Chronographo, 1189–1204 A.D. (Poem.) 624–46.

j. Constantinopolis expugnata, 1202–1204 A.D. (Poem.)   646–61.

Tome II (Paris 1881).

The whole volume includes historical and philological notes on the texts mentioned in the first volume. Two Greek texts, however, are reproduced in a special appendix without translation into Latin.

a. Nicetae Choniatae Oratio inedita.   737–41.
b. Ex Theodori Prodromi Carminibus ineditis. (Copious indices follow at end of volume.)   741–74.

ADDITIONAL NOTES

1. The *Alexiad* of Anna Comnena should be studied in the complete editions with translations in several languages. Consult A. Reifferscheid, 2 vols., Leipzig 1884; B. Leib, 3 vols., Paris 1937; English trans. by E. A. S. Dawes, London 1928.

2. Other sources:

Attaliates, Michael: *Historia,* ed. by I. Bekker (*Corpus Script.*), Bonn 1853.

Choniates, Nicetas: *Historia,* ed. by I. Bekker (*Corpus Script.*) Bonn 1935; also in *Patr. Gr.,* CXXXIX.

Cinnamus, John: *Historia,* ed. by I. Meineke (*Corpus Script.*), Bonn 1838; also in *Patr. Gr.,* CXXXIII.

Ephraemius Monachus, ed. by I. Bekker (*Corpus Script.*), Bonn 1840.

Gregoras, Nicephoras: *Historia Byzantina,* ed. by L. Schopen (*Corpus Script.*), Bonn 1829–35.

Martinov, J.: *Dernières publications relatives aux Croisades et à l'Orient Latin,* Paris 1880. (Also see A. Vasiliev: *History of the Byzantine Empire,* in 1 vol., Madison, Wisc., 1952; and L. Bréhier: *Le Monde byzantin,* III, Paris 1948–49.)

Psellus, Michael: "Chronographia," ed. by C. Sathas, *Bibliographia Graeca Medii Aevi,* Paris 1874; French trans. by Furcy Reinaud: *Chronographie ou histoire d'un siècle de Byzance (976–1077),* 2 vols., Paris 1926–28.

E. Documents Arméniens
2 vols.

Tome I (Paris 1869). Ed. Dulaurier.

1. Introduction (xvii–cxxiv): Le Royaume de la Petite-Arménie, ou La Cilicie au temps des Croisades. (An elaborate account in three chapters followed by full chronological tables of the Armenian dynasties as well as the Turcoman emirs of Cappadocia; includes Vahram Rabuni of Edessa and Vartan of Gandzak.)

2. Extraits de la Chronique de Matthieu d'Édesse. (Original Armenian and French translation. Beginning with the expeditions of Nicephoras Phocas and John Zimisces in Mesopotamia, Syria, and Palestine in the year 936 A.D. and ending in 1137 A.D.) 4–150.

3. Chronique de Grégoire le Prêtre. (This is a continuation of Matthew of Edessa's "Chronicle." Begins where his predecessor left off in 1137 A.D. and closes in 1163 A.D.) 152–201.

4. Oraison funèbre de Baudouin, comte de Marasch et de Kéçoun, par Basile, docteur en théologie, son confesseur. (Basil, according to Gregory the Priest, died in the year 611 of the Armenian era, i.e., between Feb. 9, 1162 and Feb. 8, 1163.) 204–22.

5. Élégie sur la prise d'Édesse, par Saint Nersès Schnorhali (le gracieux). (Poem in original Armenian with French translation. The author died at the age of seventy-five in the year 621 of the Armenian era/1172 A.D.) 226–68.

6. Élégie du patriarche Grégoire Dgha, Catholicos d'Arménie, neveu (fils de frère) du seigneur Nersès, notre (précédent) Catholicos, sur la prise de Jérusalem (par Saladin). (He died in May 1189 at the age of fifty-seven after sixteen years in the pontificate; he was a contemporary of Frederick Barbarossa in Cilicia and former envoy to Saladin.) 272–307.

7. Extrait de la Chronique de Michel le Syrien. (Jacobite patriarch of Antioch, and the hundredth in their line of succession, Michael died in the year 1511 of the Greek era [1199–1200 A.D.] at the age of seventy-three, after thirty-three years in the pontificate. Extract covering years 1011 to c. 1205 A.D.) 311–409.

8. Extrait de l'Histoire d'Arménie de Guiragos de Kantzag. (An Armenian monk, Kirakos was born at the beginning of the 13th century.) 413–30.

9. Extrait de l'Histoire Universelle de Vartan le grand. (Vartan's history starts with the creation and ends in 1269 A.D. He used Matthew of Edessa and Michael the Syrian. Extract covers years 1163–1221 A.D.) 434–43.

10. Extrait de la Chronographie de Samuel d'Ani. (A priest, Samuel wrote concerning the period from the creation to 1178 A.D., following the example of Eusebius.) 447–68.

11. Table chronologique de Héthoum, comte de Gorigos. (Covers years 1076–1308 A.D.) 471–90.

12. Chronique rimée des rois de la Petite-Arménie, par le docteur Vahram d'Édesse. (Begins c. 1040 and ends c. 1280 A.D.) 492–535.

13. Chant populaire sur la captivité de Léon, fils du roi Héthoum Ier. (Commemorating the defeat and captivity of the king by the Mamluk sultan Baybars in the year 1266 A.D.) 539–40.

14. Poème de Héthoum I, roi d'Arménie. (A king caught between Mongols, Egyptians, and Crusaders, his reign was often interrupted and finally came to an end in 1305 A.D. Poem reflects the times.) 550–55.

15. Extraits de l'ouvrage intitulé Réflexions sur les institutions de l'église et explication du mystère de la messe, par Saint Nersès de Lampron. (Written in 1177 A.D., preceded by long introduction on the saint and his writings.) 569–603.

16. Chronique du royaume de la Petite Arménie, par le connétable Sempad. (Covers the years 1092–1335 A.D. Preceded by a long notice in French on Sempad and his work and followed by an appendix, pp. 673–80, in Armenian and French, on the ecclesiastical and military hierarchy.) 611–72.

17. Liste rimée des souverains de la Petite Arménie, par Mardiros de Crimée. (Describes the Armenian line from the extinction of the kingdom of Cilicia to the kingdom of the Lusignans in Cyprus in 1375.) 684–87.

18. Relation de la Conférence tenue entre le docteur Mekhithâr de Daschir, envoyé de Catholicos Constantin Ier, et le légat du Pape à Saint-Jean d'Acre, en 1262. (Throws light on the

approach between the Armenian and Latin Churches.)
692–98.

The volume ends with an Appendix (697–744) in French only,
entitled "Continuation et fin de l'histoire du royaume de la
Petite Arménie," covering the period from 1339 A.D. to 1405 A.D.
and describing the Lusignan descendants until the extinction of
all traces of the Armenian lineage. Contains a series of Armenian
charters with some facsimiles.   745–62.

Tome II (Paris 1906).
Dulaurier, Schéfer, de Mas Latrie, Riant, Kohler.

1. Introduction by Ch. Kohler (v–cclxiv). (Long detailed account of the six authors included in this volume with their
work. Note that the chronicles and tracts in this volume appear mainly in French and Latin, unlike the original sources
in the first volume, where the Armenian texts are systemati-
cally published with a French translation. The new documents, originating mainly outside Armenia, appear in the
Middle French and Latin of their environment.)

2. Chronique d'Arménie par Jean Dardel. (From 1377 A.D.
Dardel was confessor and secretary of Léon V de Lusignan,
last Armenian king. In 1383 Dardel became bishop of Tortiboli in the see of Benevento. He was the official histori-
ographer of the king. His "Chronicle" extends to 1384 A.D.)
2–109.

3. Hayton: La flor des estoires de la terre d'Orient. (Of Armenian royal descent, Hayton [Hetoum] lived and wrote in the
first half of the 14th century. His work is particularly important on the Tartars in Cathay, on Northern China, and
on Central Asia.)   113–523.

4. Haytonus: Flos Historiarum Terre Orientis. (Latin version
of the above work.)   255–363.

5. Brocardus: Directorium ad passagium faciendum. (Published
along with the Middle French translation entitled "Brochard:
L'advis directif pour faire le passage d'oultremer," described
as the "Pseudo-Brocardus." The work was submitted to
Philip VI of France in 1332 A.D. for propagandist purposes.)
367–517.

6. Guillelmus Adae: De mode sarracenos extirpandi. (Guil-

laume Adam, a Dominican, later archbishop of Sultaniya, formulated this Crusade project and dedicated it to Cardinal Raimond de Farge, Clement V's nephew, in 1310 A.D.) 521–55.

7. Daniel de Thaurisio: Responsio Fratris Danielis ad errores impositos Hermenis. (Written about 1341 by Daniel, who was a Franciscan in the cathedral church of Sīs, on the subject of uniting the Armenian Church with the Roman See, a subject vigorously discussed in the 14th century.) 559–650.

8. Les Gestes des Chiprois.

    i. Livre I. Chronique de Terre Sainte (1132–1224). 653–69.

    ii. Livre II. Estoire de la guerre qui fu entre l'empéreur et Johan d'Ibelin (1228–1243). (Wars fought in defense of the rights of Henry I de Lusignan of Cyprus against the pretensions of Emperor Frederick II.) 670–736.

    iii. Livre III. (This third book is a continuation of the other two, from 1243 A.D. to the beginning of the 14th century. The author of the first two books is known to be Philippe de Novare (Philip of Novara). The third author is anonymous, but it is suggested that he may be identified as Gérard de Montréal, a Cypriot knight mentioned in the chronicles of Amadi and Bustrone. Novare recorded what he heard, but Montréal wrote what he witnessed—hence the high value of his accounts.) 737–872.

ADDITIONAL NOTES

1. Armenian sources:

Aristaces of Lastivert: *History* (Armenian text, prior to Crusades c. 1000–1064 A.D.), Venice 1844.

Asolik, Stephen of Toron: *11th Century Universal History* (Armenian text), Paris 1859, St. Petersburg 1885; Russian trans., Moscow 1864.

King Hetoum II (d. 1305): *Short Chronicle of Kingdom of Cilicia* (Armenian, published with Armenian Bible), Amsterdam 1666, Constantinople 1705, and Venice 1733.

Kirakos of Ganzag: *History*, French trans. by M. F. Brosset, St. Petersburg 1870.

Langlois, V.: *Le Trésor des chartes d'Arménie, ou Cartulaire royale des Roupéniens,* Venice 1863.

Matthew of Edessa: *History* (Armenian text), Jerusalem 1862; fuller French trans. by E. Dulaurier, Paris 1858.

Mkhitar of Erivan: *History from the Creation to 1289* (Armenian text), Moscow 1860, and St. Petersburg 1867; French trans. by M. F. Brosset, St. Petersburg 1869.

Oberlian, Stephen, archbishop of Siuni: *History of his diocese to 1297* (Armenian text), Paris 1859, and Moscow 1861; French trans. by M. F. Brosset, St. Petersburg 1864–66.

Samuel of Ani: *12th century chronological tables to 1179 with anonymous continuation to 1340* (Latin trans.), Milan 1818, Rome 1839; French trans. by M. F. Brosset, in *Collection d'Historiens Arméniens,* II, St. Petersburg 1876.

Sebeos, bishop: *History of Heraclius to 661 A.D.* (Armenian text), Constantinople 1851, and St. Petersburg 1879; French trans. by F. Macler, Paris 1904.

Sempad: *Chronicle from 952 to 1274 with Continuation to 1331* (Armenian text), Moscow 1856, and Paris 1859; French trans. by V. Langlois, St. Petersburg 1862.

Vahram Rabuni von Edessa: "Chronique rimée des rois de la Petite Arménie," English trans. by C. F. Neumann, *Vahram's Chronicle of the Armenian Kingdom in Cilicia,* London 1831; also in *Recueil, Documents Arméniens,* I (see above).

Vartan der Grosse von Gandzak: *Vseobscaja istorija Vartana Velikago* (Histoire universelle de Vartan le grand), ed. with Russian trans. by N. O. Emin, Moscow 1864; French trans. in the publications of the Société Mekhitariste, Venice 1862; also in *Recueil, Documents Arméniens,* I (see above).

2. Syriac sources:

Budge, W. Wallis (ed. and English trans.): *Chronography by Abul Faraj (Gregory) Bar Hebraeus,* 2 vols., Oxford 1932.

Chabot, J. B.: *Chronique de Michel le Syrien,* 4 vols., Paris 1899–1910.

Lüders, A.: *Die Kreuzzüge im Urteil der syrischen und armenischen Historiker* (Dissert.), Hamburg 1953. (Covers Armenian as well as Syriac sources.)

Tritton, A. S., and H. A. R. Gibb: "The First and Second Crusades from an Anonymous Syriac Chronicle," *Journal of the
Royal Asiatic Society*, 1933, 63–101.

3. Hebrew sources:

Benjamin of Tudela: *Voyages*, ed. by Adler, London 1907.
Joseph, Rabbi: *The Chronicles of Joseph Ben Joshua Ben Meir,
the Sphardi*, trans. from Hebrew by C. H. F. Bialloblotsky, 2
vols., London 1836.
Neubauer, A., and M. Stern (eds.) : *Hebräische Berichte über die
Judenverfolgungen während der Kreuzzüge (Quellen zur
Geschichte der Juden in Deutschland*, II) , Berlin 1892.

II. PALESTINE PILGRIMS' TEXT SOCIETY LIBRARY

Committee of the Palestine Exploration Fund
13 volumes, London 1890–97

Volume I (London 1896) .

A. The Churches of Constantine at Jerusalem. Translations
from Eusebius (Life of Constantine) and the Early Pilgrims,
by J. H. Bernard. Preface by C. W. Wilson; introduction,
notes, and drawings by T. Hayter Lewis. 1–38, with illustrations.

B. The Bordeaux Pilgrim (333 A.D.) . Translated from the original Latin by Aubrey Stewart; annotated by C .W. Wilson.
1–68, with maps.

C. The Pilgrimage of St. Silvia of Aquitania to the Holy Places

(c. 385 A.D.). Translated by J. H. Bernard; annotated by C. W. Wilson. 1–150, with map and illustrations.

D. The Letter of Paula and Eustochium to Marcella about the Holy Places (386 A.D.). Translated from the original Latin by A. Stewart; annotated by C. W. Wilson. 1–16.

E. The Pilgrimage of the Holy Paula, by St. Jerome (382 A.D.). Translated from the original Latin by A. Stewart; annotated by C. W. Wilson. 1–16, with map.

Volume II (London 1890–96).

A. The Epitome of St. Eucherius about Certain Holy Places (440 A.D.), and the "Breviary, or Short Description of Jerusalem" (c. 530 A.D.). Translated from the original Latin by A. Stewart; annotated by C. W. Wilson. (Eucherius was bishop of Lyons, 434–450 A.D.) 1–23.

B. Theodosius (530 A.D.). Translated from the original Latin by J. H. Bernard; annotated by C. W. Wilson. 1–20.

C. The Buildings of Justinian, by Procopius of Caesarea (c. 560 A.D.). Translated from the original Greek by A. Stewart; annotated by C. W. Wilson and T. H. Lewis. 1–178, with maps and illustrations.

D. The Holy Places Visited by Antoninus Martyr (560–70 A.D.). Translated from the original Latin by A. Stewart; annotated by C. W. Wilson. 1–44 with a map.

Volume III (London 1893–96).

A. The Pilgrimage of Arculfus (c. 670 A.D.). Translated from the original Latin and annotated by J. R. Macpherson. (Arculfus was a French bishop. His itinerary is followed by a Supplement, containing a tract entitled "A Little Book Concerning the Holy Places, which Bede composed by abbreviating the Works of the Former Writer.") 1–64, with illustrations.

B. The Hodoeporicon of St. Willibald (c. 754 A.D.). Translated from the original Latin by W. R. Brownlow, bishop of Clifton; followed by the "Itinerary of St. Willibald." (Willibald was the first English pilgrim and the son of an English king.) 1–58, with 2 maps.

C. al-Muqaddasi (al-Maqdisi): Description of Syria, including

Palestine, by al-Mukaddasi (Shams-al-dīn Muḥammad ibn Aḥmad) (c. 895 A.D.). Translated from the Arabic and annotated by Guy LeStrange. 1–116, with map. Appendix, 99–103, contains further notes by G. W. Wilson.

D. The Itinerary of Bernard the Wise (870 A.D.). Translated from the original Latin by J. H. Bernard. 1–12. Followed, 12–14, by a tract (c. 1090 A.D.?) entitled "How the City of Jerusalem is situated."

Volume IV (London 1893–96).

A. Diary of a Journey through Syria and Palestine, by Nasir-i-Khusrau (d. 1060 A.D.). Translated from the Persian and annotated by Guy LeStrange. 1–72, with maps.

B. The Pilgrimage of Saewulf (1103 A.D.). Translated by W. R. Brownlow, lord bishop of Clifton. Illustrated, with a facsimile from the original MS. 1–55, with map and plans.

C. The Pilgrimage of the Russian abbot Daniel in the Holy Land (1106–7 A.D.). Annotated by C. W. Wilson. (The original text in Russian has been translated into French, Greek, and German. This English version is made from Mme. Sophie de Khitrowo's French translation published by the Société de l'Orient Latin.) 1–108, with illustrations.

Volume V (London 1896).

A. Fretellus, archdeacon of Antioch (c. 1130 A.D.). Translated from the original Latin and annotated by J. R. Macpherson. 1–58, with map.

B. Description of the Holy Land, by John of Würzburg (1160–70 A.D.). Translated from the original Latin by A. Stewart; annotated by C. W. Wilson. 1–72, with map.

C. The Pilgrimage of Joannes Phocas (1185 A.D.). Translated from the original Greek by A. Stewart. (A native of Crete, Phocas served in the army of Manuel Comnenus, married, then retired to monasticism and made his pilgrimage as a monk.) 1–36.

D. Description of the Holy Places, by Theoderick (c. 1172 A.D.). Translated from the original Latin by A. Stewart. 1–86, with plan of Jerusalem.

E. Two letters: One from Sir Joseph de Cancy, Knight Hospitaller, to King Edward I (1281 A.D.); and One from King Edward I to Sir Joseph. Communicated to the Palestine Pilgrims' Text Society by W. B. Sanders from Champollion-Figeac's French collection of "Lettres des Rois et des Reines." 1–16.

Volume VI (London 1894–96).

A. Anonymous Pilgrims, I–VIII. Translated by A. Stewart. Pilgrim VI, 37–69, is designated as "Pseudo-Beda." 1–86.
B. The City of Jerusalem (C. 1220 A.D.). Translated from the Old French with notes by C. R. Conder. (Based on the "Citez de Jhérusalem" written after Saladin's conquest of the city in 1187 A.D., and supplemented by the "Account of Palestine" by Ernoul about 1231 A.D.) 1–69, with plan of Jerusalem and map of Syria.
C. Guide-Book to Palestine (1350 A.D.). Translated from the original Latin by J. H. Bernard. (Ms. preserved in the Library of Trinity College, Dublin.) 1–44.
D. Description of the Holy Land, by John Poloner (c. 1421 A.D.). Translated from Tobler's Text by A. Stewart. 1–52.

Volumes VII–X, in 4 parts (London 1893–96).

The Book of Wanderings of Brother Felix Fabri (1480–84 A.D.). Translated from the original Latin of Fabri's "Evagatorium," with map and plan. (Felix was a friar from the Dominican convent at Ulm. He made the journey twice to the Holy Land.)

Volume XI (London 1895–96).

A. Extracts from Aristeas; Hecataeus of Abdera; Origen's Treatise against Celsius; Lectures of St. Cyril; the Life of St. Saba; Dion Cassius; Paschal Chronicle; the Patriarch Sophronius; the Chronicle of Theophanes; and the Eutychii Annales. Translated from the original texts by A. Stewart. 1–70.
B. Jacques de Vitry: History of Jerusalem (1180 A.D.). Part of the abbreviated history translated from the original Latin by A. Stewart.

Volume XII (London 1895–96).

A. Burchard of Mount Sion (1280 A.D.). Translated from the original Latin by A. Stewart, with geographical notes by C. R. Conder. 1–111.

B. Part XIV of Bk. III of Marino Sanuto's "Secrets for True Crusaders to Help them to Recover the Holy Land" (1321 A.D.). Translated from the original Latin by A. Stewart, with geographical notes by C. R. Conder. 1–73, with 3 maps.

C. Ludolph von Suchem's "Description of the Holy Land" (1350 A.D.). Translated from the Latin by A. Stewart. 1–142.

Volume XIII (London 1897).

The life of Saladin, by Beha ed-Din. Work entitled "What Befell Salah-al-Din," 1137–93 A.D., composed by Baha-al-Din ibn Shaddad. Translated from the French version in the *Recueil* and compared with the Arabic text by C. R. Conder. 1–420, with 5 maps. Followed by General Index.

ADDITIONAL NOTES

1. Cf. Atiya: *Crusade, Commerce and Culture,* 000; Röhricht: *Bibliotheca Geographica Palaestina* (see below, General Bibliography, section IV.9) ; and H. Mayer: *Bibliographie zur Geschichte der Kreuzzüge,* Munich 1960, nos. 1751–97.

2. Other Pilgrim collections include the following significant materials:

L'An Mille—Oeuvres de Liutprand, Raoul Glaber, Adhémar de Chabannes, Adalbéron, Helgaud, réunies, traduites et présentées par E. Pognon, Paris 1947.

Itinera hierosolymitana et descriptiones Terrae Sanctae bellis sacris anteriora et latina lingua exarata, ed. by Titus Tobler and Augustus Molinier (Soc. Or. Lat., *Sér. Géog.*), 2 vols., Geneva 1879–85; Vol. I issued in 2 pts., 1877–79; Vol. II, pt. 1, ed. by A. Molinier and C. Kohler. (Contents deal with pilgrims, pilgrim voyages, historical geography of Palestine, and descriptions of Jerusalem.)

Itinera hierosolymitana saeculi IV–VIII, ed. by P. Geyer (*Corpus Scriptorum Ecclesiasticorum Latinorum,* XXXIX), Vienna 1898.

Itinéraires à Jérusalem et descriptions de la Terre Sainte, redigés en français aux XIe, XIIe et XIIIe siècles, publiés par H.

Michelant et G. Raynaud (Soc. Or. Lat., *Sér. Géog.*), Geneva 1892.

Itinéraires Russes en Orient, French trans. by Mme. de Khitrowo (Soc. Or. Lat., *Sér. Géog.*), Geneva 1889.

III. ARCHIVES DE L'ORIENT LATIN

Publiées sous le patronage de la Société de l'Orient Latin
2 volumes, Paris 1881–84, ed. by Comte Riant

Tome I (1881).

A. Critique des sources.
   I. Comte Riant (ed.) : Inventaire critique des lettres historiques de Croisades. 1–224.
   II. W. A. Neumann: La Descriptio Terrae Sanctae de Bernardo d'Ascoli (1112–1120). 225–29.
   III. M. Schwab: Al-Harizi et ses pérégrinations en Terre Sainte (vers 1217). 231–44.
B. Inventaire et descriptions de manuscrits—bibliographie.
   I. Comte Riant: Inventaire sommaire des manuscrits d'Éracles. 247–56.
   II. Dépouillement des tomes XXI–XXII de l'Orbis christianus de Henri de Suarez (Paris Bibliothèque Nationale, Latin 8983–8985). Patriarcats de Jérusalem et d'Antioche. 267–87.
   III. I. Giorgi: Description du Liber bellorum Domini. (Vat. R. Chr. 547). 289–322.
   IV. W. A. Neumann: Description du manuscrit 20 H.39 de

la bibliothèque du prince de Metternich à Königswart (Variantes d'Arculf) . 323–33.

V. A. Molinier: Description de deux manuscrits contenant la règle de la Militia Passionis Christi de Philippe de Mézières. 335–64.

VI. L. de Clercq: Inventaire d'une collection de photographies executées dans le cours d'un voyage en Orient (1859–60) . 365–71.

C. Documents.

   I. Lettres.

      1. Lettre du clerc Nicétas à Constantin VII Porphyrogénète sur le feu sacré (avril 947) . 375–82.

      2. Six lettres relatives aux croisades. 383–92.

  II. Chartes.

      1. L. Viellard (ed.) : Charte relative à Pierre l'Hermite (1100) . 393–94.

      2. D. Gaëtano Tononi (ed.) : Actes constatant la présence des Plaisançais à la Ière Croisade. 395–401.

      3. R. Röhricht (ed.) : Acte de soumission des barons du royaume de Jérusalem à Frédéric II (7 mai 1241) . 402–03.

      4. Comte Riant (ed.) : Indulgences octroyées par Galerand, évêque de Beryte (1245) . 404–05.

      5. L. de Mas Latrie (ed.) : Traités des Vénitiens avec l'émir d'Acre en 1304. 406–08.

      6. J. Delaville LeRoulx (ed.) : Trois chartes du XIIe siècle concernant l'Ordre de S. Jean de Jérusalem. 409–15.

      7. Comte Riant (ed.) : Privilèges octroyés aux Teutoniques. 416–22.

      8. J. Delaville LeRoulx (ed.) : Titres de l'hôpital des Brétons d'Acre. 423–33.

      9. Chev. C. Desimoni (ed.) : Actes passés en 1271, 1274 et 1279 à l'Aïas (Petite Arménie) et à Beyrouth par devant des notaires génois. 434–534.

    10. A. de Barthélemy (ed.) : Libre exercice de Commerce octroyé à un pèlerin champénois (1153) . 535–36.

    11. J. Roman (ed.) : Charte de départ du dauphin Humbert II. 537–38.

12. P. Durrieu (ed.) : Procès-verbal du martyre de quatre frères mineurs en 1391. 539–46.

III. Poèmes.

1. W. Wattenbach (ed.) : Le Solymarius de Gunther de Paris. 551–61.

2. Marquis de Vogüé (ed.) : Achard d'Arrouaise, Poème sur le Templum Domini. 562–79.

3. H. Hagenmeyer (ed.) : Deux poésies latines relatives à la IIIe Croisade. 580–85.

IV. Documents divers.

1. Ch. Schéfer: Aboul Hasan Aly el Herewy. Indications sur les lieux de pèlerinage (extraits). 587–609.

2. P. Viollet: Les remembrances de la Haute Cour.—Les Usages de Naxos. 610–14.

D. Mélanges Historiques et Archéologiques.

I. R. Röhricht: Études sur les derniers temps du royaume de Jérusalem. (a) La croisade du prince Édouard d'Angleterre (1270–74). 617–32. (b) Les batailles de Hims (1281 et 1291). 633–52.

II. L. de Mas Latrie: Projets d'empoisonnements de Mahomet II et du pacha de Bosnie accueillis par la république de Venise. 653–62.

III. G. Schlumberger: Trois sceaux et deux monnaies de l'époque des croisades. 633–78.

IV. ———: Bulles de hauts fonctionnaires de l'ordre militaire. 679–96.

V. A. Mordtmann: Bulles byzantines relatives aux Varègues. 697–703.

VI. Comte Riant: Les archives des établissements Latins d'Orient à propos d'une publication récente de l'École de Rome. 705–10.

Tome II (1884), Part 1.

A. Critique des sources.

I. U. Robert: La Chronique d'Arménie de Jean Dardel, évêque de Tortiboli. 1–15.

II. H. Hagenmeyer: Étude sur la Chronique de Zimmern; renseignements qu'elle fournit sur la première croisade. 17–88.

III. Ch. Schéfer: Étude sur la Devise des chemins de Babilonie. 89–101.

B. Inventaires et descriptions de manuscrits.

  I. Comte Riant: Inventaire des matériaux rassemblés par les Bénédictins au XVIIIe siècle pour la publication des Historiens des Croisades. 105–30.

  II. ———: Inventaire sommaire des manuscrits relatifs à l'histoire et à la géographie de l'Orient Latin. I, 131–204; II, 510–12.

C. Mélanges historiques et archéologiques.

  I. L. de Mas Latrie: Histoire des archevêques latins de l'île de Chypre. 207–328.

  II. E. G. Rey: Les périples des côtes de Syrie et de la Petite Arménie. 331–53.

  III. W. Heyd: Les Consulats établis en Terre Sainte au Moyen-Age pour la protection des pèlerins. I, 355–63; II, 512.

  IV. R. Röhricht: Études sur les derniers temps du royaume de Jérusalem. Les combats du Sultan Bibars contre les chrétiens en Syrie (1261–77). 365–406.

  V. Comte Riant: Invention de la sépulture des patriarches Abraham, Isaac et Jacob à Hébron le 25 juin 1119. I, 411–21; II, 512–13.

  VI. G. Schlumberger: Sigillographie byzantine des ducs et catépans d'Antioche, des patriarches d'Antioche et des ducs et catépans de Chypre. 423–38.

  VII. J. B. de Rossi: Verre representant le Temple de Jérusalem. 439–55.

  VIII. Clermont-Ganneau: Nouveaux Monuments des Croisés recueillis en Terre Sainte. I, 457–64; II, 513–14.

Tome II (1884), Part 2. Documents.

I. Chartes.

  1. Chev. C. Desimoni (ed.): Actes passées à Famagouste de 1299 à 1301 par devant le notaire génois Lamberto di Sambuceto. 3–120.

  2. Comte de Marsy (ed.): Fragment d'un cartulaire de l'ordre de Saint Lazare en Terre Sainte. 121–57.

3. Documents concernant les seigneurs de Ham, connétables de Tripoli 1227–28.   158–63.

4. J. de Zahn (ed.) : Quatre piéces relatives à l'Ordre Teutonique en Orient.   164–69.

5. L. de Mas Latrie (ed.) : Documents génois concernant l'histoire de Chypre.   170–76.

6. L. Demaison (ed.) : Documents relatifs à une relique de Saint Philippe, rapportée de Terre Sainte à Saint-Remi de Rheims.   177–83.

7. A. de Barthélemy (ed.) : Chartes de départ et de retour des comtes de Dampierre-en-Astenois (IVe et Ve croisades).   184–207.

8. G. Tononi (ed.) : Documents relatifs aux Plaisançais d'Orient.   208–12.

9. Chev. C. Desimoni (ed.) : Quatre titres de propriétés des Génois à Acre et à Tyr.   213–30.

10. Chev. L. Belgrano (ed.) : Une charte de nolis de S. Louis.   231–36.

11. Comte Riant (ed.) : Pièces relatives au passage à Venise de pèlerins de Terre Sainte.   237–49.

II. Lettres.

1. S. Löwenfeld (ed.) : Documents relatifs à la croisade de Guillaume, comte de Ponthieu.   251–55.

2. Comte Riant (ed.) : Une lettre de l'impératrice Marie de Constantinople.   256–57.

3. R. Röhricht (ed.) : Lettres de Ricoldo de Monte-Croce sur la prise d'Acre (1291).   258–96.

4. W. Wattenbach (ed.) : Fausse correspondance du sultan avec Clement V.   297–302.

III. Voyages.

1. G. A. Neumann (ed.) : Ludolphus von Sudheim, De itinere Terre Sancte.   305–77.

2. Comte Riant (ed.) : Voyage en Terre Sainte d'un Maire de Bordeaux au XIVe siècle.   378–88.

3. R. P. J. Martinov (ed.) : Récit sur les lieux saints de Jérusalem, traduit d'un texte slavon du XIVe siècle.   389–93.

4. P. L. Alishan (ed.) : Deux descriptions arméniennes des Lieux Saints de Palestine.   394–403.

    (i) Anastase d'Arménie (VIIe siècle), Les lxx couvents arméniens de Jérusalem.

    (ii) Nicolas d'Acquirmann (1483), Les ss. Lieux de Jérusalem.

IV. Textes divers.

  1. C. Sathas (ed.) : Vies des saints allemands de l'église de Chypre. 405–26.

  2. R. Röhricht and G. Raynaud (eds.) : Annales de Terre Sainte. 427–61.

  3. R. Röhricht and I. Guidi: Gabriel Bar Kalâ'i, évêque de Nicosie, Poème sur la chute de Tripoli, 27 avril 1289. 462–66.

  4. P. Meyer (ed.) : Fragment d'une chanson d'Antioche provençal. 467–509.

IV. EXUVIAE SACRAE CONSTANTINOPOLITANAE

Fasciculus documentorum minorum, ad byzantina lipsana in Occidentem saeculo XIII° translata, spectantium and Historiam Quarti Belli Sacri imperii; gallo-graeci illustrantium. 3 tomes.

Tome I (Geneva 1877)

Preface (xii–ccxxii).—Long discussion on (1) Sources of the Fourth Crusade. (2) Transportation of the religious relics from Constantinople to the West. (3) Examination of liturgical and diverse documents, letters, and charters.

Documenta Hagiographica:

A. Acta Translationum.

    i. Anonymi Suessionensis, De terra Iherosolimi tana et quomodo ad urbe Constantinopolitane ad hanc ecclesiam allate sunt reliquie. 3–9.

    ii. Anonymi Halberstadensis, De peregrinatione in Greciam et adventu relliquiarum de Greceia libellus. 10–21.

    iii. Canonici Lingonensis, Historia translationum relliquiarum S. Mamantis. 22–34.

    iv. Rigardi de Gerboredo, De capta et direpta a Latinis Constantinopoli et quomodo Walo caput S. Iohannis Baptiste invenit et ad Ambianum deportavit, cum Roberti Viseur versione gallica. 35–44.

    v. Gualterii Cornuti, Historia susceptionis Corone spinee. 45–56.

B. Relationes Coevae.

    i. Guntheri Parisiensis, Historia Constantinopolitana, seu de expugnatione urbis Constantinopolitane, unde, inter alias reliquias, magne pars S. Crucis in Alemanniam est allata. 57–126.

    ii. Rostangni Cluniacensis Monachi, Narratio exceptionis, apud Cluniacum, capitis S. Clementis, ex ore Dalmacij de serciaco, militis, excepta. 127–140.

    iii. Monachi S. Georgii, Translatio corporis beatissimi Pauli Martyris, de Constantinopoli Venetias. 141–149.

    iv. Anonymi Caietani, Qualiter caput S. Theodori ad Caietam translatum est. 150–155.

    v. Translatio corporis beatissimi Theodori, martyris Heraclaensis, cum multis miraculis, cum versione italica. 156–163.

C. Narrationes Aetate Inferiores.

    i. Matthei Amalphitani, Translatio corporis S. Andree de Constantinopoli in Amalphiam. 166–178.

    ii. Petri Calo, Translationes II. 179–183.

       a. Translatio S. Iohannis Alexandrini.

       b. Translatio S. Barbare.

    iii. Translationes II Venetianae Minores. 184–188.

       a. Corporis b. virginis ac martiris Lucie, Venetias ex Constantinopoli urbe, translatio.

       b. Translatio corporis beatissimi Pauli protoeremite.

iv. Narrationum II deperditarum versiones Gallicae recentiones. 184–196.
  a. Histoire de la Saincte-Larme de N.S. Jésus-Christ, apportée de Constantinople à l'abbaye de Sélincourt, par Bernard de Moreuil.
  b. Narré Touchant la Saincte-Croix de l'abbaye du Mont Saint-Quentin.

Tome II (Geneva 1878)

Documenta Liturgica.   3–50.

Epistolae et Instrumenta ad Exuvias Constantinopolitanas in Occidentem Translatas Spectantia. (Epistles numbering 144 and ranging from the year 1204 to 1498.)   54–172.

Documenta Diversa. (Including inscriptions, necrologies, rites, and church inventories.)   175–200.

Appendix. (Comprising recorded testimonies of transfer of holy relics from Constantinople in the 13th century to France, Belgium, Italy, Germany, England, and Scandinavia.)   203–88.

Kalendarium Festorum, Reliquias Constantinopolitanas, in Occidentem Saeculo XIII Translatas, Commemorantium. (Tables of the days of saints whose relics were translated to the West, with details of where they rested and when they were translated, as well as the witnesses thereof.)   289–302.

Tome III (Paris 1904).

Notes et études archéologiques, by F. de Mély.

Volume comprises three illustrated archaeological treatises:
  1. La croix des premiers croisés.   1–21.
  2. La sainte lance.   23–163.
  3. La couronne d'épines.   165–440.

V. BIBLIOTHÈQUE DES CROISADES

4 volumes, Paris 1829

Compiled by J. F. Michaud as a supplement to his *Histoire des Croisades,* this was probably the first serious attempt at a comprehensive documentary record drawn from almost all the known sources on the Crusades. Though nearly a century and a half old, this work is still of considerable use as a starting point; and an analysis of its contents is quite justifiable. In reality, the idea of the *Bibliothèque* must have played a capital role in the organization of the more monumental collection of the *Recueil des Historiens des Croisades,* which it preceded and on whose committee Michaud was a prominent member. The author followed the analytical system in dealing with his sources, but he also freely made copious excerpts from the original texts. The fourth part of the series, devoted to the Arabic chronicles, was essentially the work of M. Reinaud, one of the early French Arabists, who translated and organized the whole volume for Michaud. Reinaud, who filled a curatorial function in the cabinet of Oriental manuscripts of the king of France, then became one of the pillars of the Arabic historians' series in the *Recueil.*

Part I. Chroniques de France

Here the author analyzed five collections of chronicles, followed by additional notices and detailed indices.

First Collection of Bongars (*Gesta Dei per Francos,* 2 vols., Hanover 1611, 1–100). This contains a survey of the following:

Tüdebode: Gesta Francorum. 2–3.

Robert le Moine: Historia hierosolymita. 3–19.

Baudri, archbishop of Dol: Historia hierosolymitana. 9–16.

Raimond d'Agiles: Historia hierosolymitanae expeditionis. 43–81.

Foucher de Chartres: Gesta peregrinantium Francorum cum armis Hierusalem pergentium. 82–96.

Anonymous: Gesta Francorum expugnantium Hierusalem. 96–99.

Anonymous: second part (first part lost) of the Historiae hierosolymitanae. 99–104.

Gauthier le Chancelier: Bella Antiochena. 104–25.

Guibert: Gesta Dei per Francos. 125–33.

Guillaume, archbishop of Tyre: Historia rerum in partibus transmarinis gestarum a tempore successorum Mahometis usque ad annum Domini 1184. 131–68.

Jacques de Vitri, bishop of Acre: Historia hierosolymitana. 168–81.

Geoffroi Vinisauf: Historia hierosolymitana. 181.

Letters of princes and kings. 182–85.

Letter of Olivier, scholastique de Cologne. 185.

Bull of Innocent IV. 185–86.

Canonization of St. Louis, king of France. 186–87.

Marino Sanudo: Liber secretorum fidelium crucis super Terrae-sanctae recuperatione et conservatione, quo et Terrae-Sanctae historia ab origine et ejusdem vicinarumque provinciarum geographica descriptio continetur. 188–98.

Anonymous: De recuperatione Terrae-sanctae, auctor anonymus. (Author was the attorney of the king of England to the duchy of Aquitaine.) 198–99.

Second Collection of André and François Duchesne (*Historiae francorum scriptores coaetanei, ab ipsius gentis origine ad Philippi IV dicti Pulchri tempora, cum Epistolis Regum, Reginarum, Pontificum, Ducum, Comitum, Abbatum, et aliis veteribus rerum Francicarum monumentis,* 5 vols., Paris 1639–49). An old monumental work, this collection comprises most of the French historians of the time, from the origins to the reign of Philippe IV, coupled with a series of original documents from all sources. The following is a quick survey of the contents, together with reference to both Duchesne and the *Bibliothèque des Croisades* of Michaud:

Raoul Glaber, monk of Cluny: Historiarum sui temporis Libri V, ab electione Hugonis Capeti in regem, ad annum usque MXLVI. (Duchesne, III, 1 ff; *Bibliothèque*, I, 201–04.)

Anonymous fragment: Historiae Francicae Fragmentum, a Roberto ad mortem Philippi I regis. (Duchesne, IV, 85 ff; *Bibliothèque*, I, 206–08.)

Suger, abbot of Saint-Denis: Vita Ludovici VI regis, qui Grossus dictus. (Duchesne, IV, 281 ff; *Bibliothèque*, I, 209.)

Teulfe and other monks of Morigni: Chronicon Morigniacensis monasterii ab anno 1108 usque ad annum 1147, quo rex Ludovicus VII in Terram-Sanctam profectus est. (Duchesne, IV, 359 ff; *Bibliothèque*, I, 209–11.)

Gesta Ludovici VII regis, filii Ludovici Grossi. (Duchesne, IV, 390 ff; *Bibliothèque*, I, 212–28.)

History attributed to Suger: Historia gloriosi regis Ludovici filii Ludovici Grossi. (Duchesne, IV, 412 ff; *Bibliothèque*, I, 245.)

Monk of the abbey of Fleuri or Saint-Bénoît-sur-Loire: Fragmentum historicum ex veteri membrana de tributo Floriacensibus impositi. (Duchesne, IV, 423 ff; *Bibliothèque*, I, 246–48.)

Letters from the reign of Louis le Gros: Epistolae historicae quae ad res Ludovici Grossi et ejus filii Ludovici Junioris regum illustrandas pertinent. (Duchesne, IV, 444–556; *Bibliothèque*, I, 349–52.)

Pierre Tudebode: Historia de hierosolymitano itinere. (Duchesne, IV, 777 ff; *Bibliothèque*, I, 252–60.)

Poem attributed to Foulques and Gilon of Paris: Historia gestorum viae nostri temporis hierosolymitanae. (Duchesne, IV, 890; *Bibliothèque*, I, 260–65.)

Rigord, the royal chronographer: Gesta Philippi Augusti Francorum regis. (Duchesne, V, 1 ff; *Bibliothèque*, I, 277–83.)

Guillaume le Breton, continuator of Rigord and royal chaplain: Historia de vita et gestis Philippi-Augusti Francorum regis. (Duchesne, V, 68 ff; *Bibliothèque*, I, 283–85.)

Friar Guillaume de Nangis, monk of Saint-Denis: Gesta S. Ludovici noni Francorum regis. (Duchesne, V, 326 ff; *Bibliothè-que*, I, 285–93.)

Miscellaneous documents on St. Louis. (Duchesne, V, 440 ff; *Bibliothèque*, I, 293–305.)

Guillaume de Tripoli of the Dominican Convent at Acre in state of Saracens after Louis IX's return from Syria: Fragmentum ex libro de statu Sarracenorum post Ludovici regis de Syria reditum. (Duchesne, V, 432 ff; *Bibliothèque*, I, 305–10.)

Miscellaneous, somewhat imperfect letters collected by Duchesne and analyzed by Michaud. (*Bibliothèque*, I, 321–26.)

Other documents, not in Duchesne, but inserted by Michaud, include:

Chronicle of Adémar de Chabannes, monk of Saint-Cibar d'Angoulême. (*Bibliothèque*, I, 205–06.)

Odo de Deuil on the voyage of St. Louis to the Orient. (*Bibliothèque*, I, 228–45.)

Pierre Angelio da Barga: "La Syriade," or expedition of Christian princes under Godefroi de Bouillon to deliver Jerusalem from Turkish tyranny. (*Bibliothèque*, I, 265–77.)

Orderic Vital: Ecclesiastical history. (*Bibliothèque*, I, 310–21.)

Third Collection by Edmond Martène and Ursin Durand (*Veterum scriptorum et monumentorum historicorum, dogmaticorum, amplissima collectio*, 9 vols., Paris 1724) . This is subdivided into two sections, of which the first is a collection of chronicles (*Bibliothèque*, I, 327–410) , and the second is entitled "Trésor des Anecdotes" (*Bibliothèque*, I, 410–36) . The chronicles cited are:

Anonymous "Gesta" of the archbishops of Trèves: Gesta Trevirensium archiepiscoporum ab anno 880 ad annum 1455. (T. IV, 142 ff; *Bibliothèque*, I, 327–41.)

Abbot Ekkard: Libellus qui dicitur Ierosolymita, de oppressione, liberatione et restauratione Ierosolimitanae ecclesiae. (T. V, 507 ff; *Bibliothèque*, I, 341–50.)

Raoul de Coggeshale, abbot of the order of Citeaux: Chronicon Terrae-Sanctae. (T. V, 543 ff; *Bibliothèque*, 351–56.)

An English chronicle: Chronicon anglicanum ab anno 1066 ad 1200. (T. V, 801 ff; *Bibliothèque*, I, 356–66.)

Continuation of Guillaume de Tyr (T. V, 581 ff; *Bibliothèque,* I, 366–77), followed by a discussion of the manuscript of Rothelin (*Bibliothèque,* I, 377–88).

Anonymous chronicle of the city of Tours: Chronicon Turonense. (T. V, 917 ff; *Bibliothèque,* I, 388–92.)

Chronicle of Richard de Poitou, monk of Cluny. (T. V, 1160 ff; *Bibliothèque,* I, 392–93.)

Michaud then devotes most of the remaining sections to letters and documents on the Crusade, with the exception of a tract on the siege of Constantinople ("Tractatus de expugnatione urbis Constantinopolis anno 1453," T. V, 785; *Bibliothèque,* I, 410), and the "Chronicle Saint-Bertin" by Jean d'Ipres, abbot of the monastery of Saint-Bertin (Chronicon Sythiense Sancti-Bertini, 590–1294 A.D., T. III, 222 ff; *Bibliothèque,* I, 410–25).

This volume of the *Bibliothèque* (I, 436–51) ends with a short analysis of a work entitled "Spicilegium, sive collectio veterum aliquot scriptorum qui in galliae bibliothecis delituerant," first edited by Luc d'Achéry, a Benedictine of the Congrégation de Saint-Maur, then re-edited, reviewed, and corrected on original manuscripts by Étienne Baluze, Edmond Martène, and Louis François-Joseph de Labarre of Tournai, in 3 vols., Paris 1723. The second volume covers the area of the Crusades and contains the following relevant chronicles:

Histoire de Trèves. 208 ff.

Chronique de saint Pierre-le-Vif de Senones de l'ordre de Saint-Benoît, by the monk Clarius. 463 ff.

Chronique de saint Médard de Soissons. 468 ff.

Chronique abrégée de Saint-Denis. 495 ff.

Histoire de l'abbaye de Senones, by Richer, monk of the same institution. 605 ff.

Chronique du monastère d'Andres dans l'évêché de Boulogne, by Abbot Guillaume, 781 ff.

The third volume, moreover, contains the Chronique de Nicolas de Treveth, dominicain (143 ff), and a number of letters and documents originally collected by d'Achéry, notably a letter from Étienne de Blois (450) dated 1098, another dated 1099 from Anselme de Ribemont to the archbishop of Rheims, and numerous documents of uneven importance.

Eight indices to the four parts of the *Bibliothèque* are presented at the close of this volume. It is of interest to note that they classify chronicles by known authors, anonymous chronicles, papal bulls, papal letters, letters by diverse personalities, historical and diplomatic documents, monumental collections and their editors, and Arabic chronicles in Part IV.

Part II. Suite des Chroniques de France; Chronique d'Italie et d'Angleterre

The first section of this volume contains a brief survey of the following collections:

Labbé, P.: *Nova Bibliotheca manuscriptorum librorum, antiquitatis praesertim Francicae monumenta,* 2 vols., Paris 1657, 465–66.

Mabillon, D. J., and D. Germain: *Museum Italicum, sive Collectio veterum scriptorum ex bibliothecis Italicis,* 2 vols., Paris 1867, 455–65.

Recueil des Historiens des Gaules et de la France, par des Religieux Benedictins, 27 vols., Paris 1738–1818, 466–87. T. XI deals with pilgrimages to the Holy Land, T. XII touches on the Crusades, T. XIII as well, and T. XV contains the register of many letters and documents of the age of the Crusades.

The second section (487 ff), devoted to the Italian chronicles and records, is based essentially on the work of L. A. Muratori: *Rerum Italicarum scriptores ab anno aerae christianae 500 ad 1500,* old ed., 25 vols. in 28, Milan 1723 ff. T. III contains the lives of popes (*Bibliothèque,* II, 488–505). The "Gesta Tancredi" occurs in T. V (285 ff; *Bibliothèque,* II, 506–25). Among other prominent features are:

Annals of Caffaro: Annales Genuenses ab anno 1100 ad annum usque 1293. (T. VI, 248 ff; *Bibliothèque,* II, 525–28.)

Otto, bishop of Frisingen: Gesta Frederici I imperatoris. (T. VI, 640 ff; *Bibliothèque,* II, 528–40.)

Otto of St.-Blaise: Chronicon ab anno 1146 usque ad annum 1209. (T. VI, 866 ff; *Bibliothèque,* II, 540–46.)

Sicardi, bishop of Cremona: Chronicon. (T. VII, 530 ff; *Bibliothèque,* II, 546–54.)

Richard of St. Germain: Chronicon. (T. VII, 968 ff; *Bibliothè-que*, 583–88.)

Anonymous Memorial of the Podestates of Reggio. (T. VIII, 1074 ff; *Bibliothèque*, II, 589–610.)

Ricoboldo di Ferrari: Istoria imperiale. From Charlemagne to Otto IV. (T. IX, 291 ff; *Bibliothèque*, II, 610–15.)

Pipin of Bologna: Chronicon. (T. IX, 583 ff; *Bibliothèque*, II, 615–17.)

Giovanni Villani: Istorie Fiorentine. (T. XII, 955; *Bibliothèque*, II, 617–25.)

Bartholomeo de Neocastro: Historia sicula a morte Friderici imper. et Siciliae regis, hoc est, ab anno 1250 ad 1294 deducta. (T. XIII, 1011 ff; *Bibliothèque*, II, 626–29.)

Marino Sanudo the Younger's lives of the doges of Venice: Vita omnium ducum. (T. XXII, 406 ff; *Bibliothèque*, II, 629–35.)

The second section also includes a series of other relatively less important chroniclers such as the anonymous monk of Padua (T. VIII, 665 ff) ; Jacob of Varagine, archbishop of Genoa (T. IX, 5 ff) ; Ptolemy of Lucca (T. IX, 754 ff) ; the anonymous authors of the Chronicle of Andrea Dandolo, doge of Venice (T. XII, 1 ff) , and the Annals of Milan (T. XVI, 637 ff) ; and others (*Bibliothèque*, II, 635–47). Michaud also interjects the French "Histoire des Croisades" by Bernard le Trésorier (*Bibliothèque*, II, 555–82) , a work of major importance for the movement.

The remainder of the second part of the *Bibliothèque* treats the following English collections on the English sources touching the Crusade. These have to be reviewed in the light of the more definitive and more recent *Rolls Series* (*Rerum Britannicarum medii aevi scriptores, or chronicles and memorials of Great Britain and Ireland during the Middle Ages,* published by the authority of Her Majesty's treasury under the direction of the Master of the Rolls, 99 vols. in 244, London 1858–1896; consult C. Gross: *The Sources and Literature of English History from the Earliest Times to about 1485,* rev. 2nd ed., N.Y. 1915) .

The collections handled by Michaud (*Bibliothèque*, II, 648, 727, 759, 779) are those edited by Thomas Gale: *Historiae anglicanae Scriptores quinque,* Oxford 1687; Roger Twisden: *Historiae Anglicanae Scriptores decem,* 2 vols., London 1652; Henry

Savile: *Rerum anglicarum scriptores post Bedam praecipui,* Frankfort 1601; and William Camden: *Anglica, Hibernica, Normannica, Cambrica, a veteribus scripta,* Frankfort 1602.

Michaud further cites the older editions of the English chroniclers, including Matthew of Westminster: *Flores Historiarum,* Frankfort 1601 (*Bibliothèque,* II, 781–92) ; Matthew of Paris: *Historia Majora,* London 1640 and 1684 (*Bibliothèque,* II, 792–845) ; and Benedict of Peterborough: *Vita et Gesta Henrici II Angliae regis,* ed. by Thomas Hearne, 2 vols., Oxford 1735 (*Bibliothèque,* II, 845–58) . The last section comprises a selection of relevant documents from the still useful collection edited by Thomas Rymer and Robert Sanderson: *Foedera, conventiones, litterae, et ejuscumque generis acta publica inter reges Angliae et alios quosvis imperatores, reges, pontifices, principes vel communitates, 1101–1654* A.D., 10 vols., Hagae Comitis 1745 (*Bibliothèque,* II, 858–85) .

Part III. Chroniques d'Allemagne et du Nord de l'Europe; Chroniques diverses; Chroniques Grecques, Turques et Arméniennes

On the German side, it will be interesting to put on record the older source collections known to Michaud and long since forgotten. These, however, should be consulted in conjunction with the modern and more definitive collections, of which the foremost is the *Monumenta Germaniae historica (500–1500* A.D.) , ed. by G. II. Pertz *et al.,* 120 vols., Hanover and Berlin 1826–1925. The fullest analysis of this monumental collection occurs as no. 892 in the Dahlmann-Waitz *Quellenkunde der deutschen Geschichte,* 1st ed. by F. C. Dahlmann, 1830; more recent and revised ed. by P. Herre *et al.,* Leipzig 1912. Other essential German source materials include *Die Chroniken der deutschen Stadte von 14. bis ins. 16 Jahrhundert,* ed. by K. Hegel and G. von Below, Leipzig 1862 ff; also analyzed in Dahlmann-Waitz, no. 1003.

Michaud used the collections of Burcard Gotthelf Struve: *Rerum Germanicorum scriptores,* 3 vols., Argentoriti, 1717 (*Bibliothèque,* III, 1–62) , and Godfredi-Guglielmi Leibnitz: *Accessiones historicae,* 2 vols., Hanover 1700 (*Bibliothèque,* III, 62–77) . Other historical collections, not closely specified, were signalled under the names H. Meibonius, F. Swertius, J. Pistorius, J. P. Ludewig, J. M. Heineccius, and J. G. Eccard (*Bibliothèque,* III, 77, 85, 87, 109, 116, 122, 126).

Frederick Barbarossa's expedition is discussed under the title "Recueil de Canisius" (*Thesaurus monumentorum et historico-rum ecclesiasticorum*) —by a contemporary writer (*Bibliothèque,* III, 160–84). A history of the capture of Constantinople in 1203–04, by Gunther, a monk of "Paris" near Basel, is quoted (*Biblio-thèque,* III, 184–92); and some German affairs in holy warfare are denoted under "Recueil de (Simon) Schardius," who died in 1573 (*Bibliothèque,* III, 192–94).

The remainder of the volume is imperfect, lacking in precise details, and insufficiently documented. But as a first exploratory attempt in a still obscure field, it is worthy of a quick glance. Under the general title of "Chroniques d'Autruche, de Bohème et de Hongrie," the *Bibliothèque* records the collections of Je-rome Pez (*Scriptores rerum Austriacarum veteres*), Wilhelm de Sommersberg (*Silesiacarum rerum scriptores*), Marquard Freher (*Rerum Bohemicarum antiqui scriptores*), Mathias Belius (*Re-rum Hungaricarum scriptores*), Joannis Thurocz (*Chronica Hun-garorum ab origine gentis*), Jacob Langebeck (*Scriptores rerum Danicarum medii aevi*), and Thermodus Torfeus (*Historiae rerum Norvegicarum*) (*Bibliothèque,* III, 194, 204, 207, 209, 210, 216, 228).

Under the title "Chroniques et Pièces Diverses" (*Bibliothè-que,* III, 233–381), a great many excerpts from miscellaneous sources are compiled in French. These include the "Chronicle" of Guillaume de Nangis, a monk of Saint-Denis; the English his-tory of Canon William Neubrig; Helmode's "Chronicle of the Slavs" and its continuation by Arnold of Lübeck: Antony Bon-fini's "History of Hungary"; the "Chronicle" of Berthold of Con-stance; the annals of the monastery of Peterhausen; the history of Thomas, archdeacon of Spalatro; the history of France by Paul Emyli of Verona: the annals of Flanders by Jacob Meyer; the Syrian war by Bizaro; and a multitude of others. The same sec-tion contains a number of official documents, such as Innocent IV's letters on the early Crusading of St. Louis, letters from Pierre de Blois, the Assises of Jerusalem on maritime law, and some manuscripts from the royal cabinet in Paris (*Bibliothèque,* III, 241–45, 250–57, 339–68, 381–84).

Then follows a series of three sets of extracts: (1) Greek historians (*Bibliothèque,* III, 385–443). These include Anna Comnena (*Alexiad*), Nicetas Choniates, and John Cinnamus, the grammarian. (2) The Turkish historian Saad-Uddin (Mohammed . . . ben-Hassan effendi, surnamed "Cogia effendi" since he was khodja or preceptor to sultans Murad III and Ahmet I, then became grand mufti of the Empire, and finally died in Constantinople in 1597). His famous history, "Taj-Uttevarikh" (Crown of histories), was written in the form of Ottoman annals. Excerpts (*Bibliothèque,* III, 444–80) are given especially for the battle of Varna (1443) and the capture of Constantinople (1453). (3) Armenian chronicles (*Bibliothèque,* III, 481–504), quoted from T. IX of the French *Notices et Extraits des manuscrits de la Bibliothèque du Roi,* Paris 1787 ff, notably from the life of St. Narsès the Great and the history of Matthew of Edessa.

Part IV. Chroniques arabes, traduites et mises en ordre par M. Reinaud, Employé au Cabinet des manuscrits orientaux de la Bibliothèque du Roi

Next to the first part of the *Bibliothèque,* this volume, despite all its shortcomings and numerous inaccuracies, remains the most valuable of the lot and may be used side by side with the *Recueil des Historiens des Croisades.* Reinaud translated for the first time directly from the Arabic manuscripts at his disposal in the royal cabinet. He did not furnish folios or pagination, which probably did not yet exist in his source material, but he made occasional excerpts in Arabic from the original texts.

The author begins with some brief notices on the Arabic chroniclers, whose works he had utilized from the Crusading angle. Thus we have a gallery of the famous names of Arabic historians whose annals contributed to building the text of both the *Bibliothèque* and the *Recueil.* These include ibn al-Athīr, Bahā' al-Dīn, 'Imad al-Dīn, Kamāl al-Dīn, Abū Shāmah, 'Abd al-Laṭif, ibn al-Jauzi, ibn Muyassir, ibn Khallikan, Yāfe'i, Jamāl

.bu al-Fidā, Abu al-Faraj the Syrian, al-Nuwairi,
bi, ibn al-Furāt, al-Maqrīzi, Abu-l-Mahāsin, al-Suyūṭi,
.l-Dīn, and the history of the Coptic patriarchs of Alexan-
as well as some anonymous treatises. (*Bibliothèque*, IV,
ii).

The whole book is composed of excerpts from the aforemen-
tioned chroniclers rendered into French and often preceded by
an analytical notice on the author or the event to be treated.
The number of these excerpts amounts to 106 and each deals
with a specific phase of Crusading history according to the best
contemporary Arabic source in Reinaud's judgment. Beginning
with the arrival of the Crusaders in Syria (1097–98) and the
seizure of Antioch, he ends with the recapture of Acre (1291) by
the Mamluk armies of Sultan al-Ashraf Khalil. Between these
dates, the full story of the Crusades is presented from the Oriental
side in the words of Arabic writers.

For the first time, the historian of the Crusades who was no
Arabic scholar could see the genesis of the movement from the
Eastern side as well as the Western. With all its defects, Reinaud's
exposition formed a base from which future generations could
forge ahead in the vast labyrinth of original Arabic materials.

VI. RECORDS OF CIVILIZATION

Columbia University Publications, 1915 to date

Ambroise: *The Crusade of Richard Lion Heart,* English trans.
from French by M. J. Hubert, notes by J. L. LaMonte, N.Y.
1941. (Cf. Ambroise: *L'Estoire de la guerre sainte,* ed. by

G. Paris [*Collection de documents inédits sur l'histoire de France*], Paris 1897.)

Dubois, Pierre: *The Recovery of the Holy Land,* English trans. from Latin with introduction and notes by Walther Brandt, N.Y. 1956.

Helmold (Helmoldus presbyter bosoviensis): *The Chronicle of the Slavs by Helmold, Priest of Bosau,* English trans. from Latin by F. J. Tschan, N.Y. 1935.

John of Salisbury: *De expugnatione Lyxbonensi* (The Conquest of Lisbon), ed. with English trans. from Latin by C. W. David, N.Y. 1936.

Lopez, R. S., and I. A. Raymond: *Medieval Trade in the Mediterranean—Illustrative Documents,* trans. with introduction and notes, N.Y. 1955.

Odo de Deuil (abbot of Saint Denis, d. c. 1162): *De profectione Ludovici VII in Orientes,* Latin text and English trans. by V. G. Berry, N.Y. 1948; earlier ed. by Migne, in *Patr. Lat.,* CLXXXV; French ed. by H. Waquet, Paris 1949.

Otto of Freising: *The Deeds of Frederick Barbarossa* (Gesta Friderici I Imperatoris), English trans. from Latin by C. C. Mierow, N.Y. 1953; text ed. by G. Waitz, Hanover 1912.

———: *The Two Cities—A Chronicle of Universal History to the Year 1146* A.D. *by Otto Bishop of Freising,* English trans. from Latin and notes by C. C. Mierow, N.Y. 1928; text ed., *M.G.H.,* XX.

Philip of Novara: *The Wars of Frederick II against the Ibelins in Syria and Cyprus, by Philip of Novara,* English trans. from French version of Ch. Kohler, which was based on the two major sources: the "Gestes des Chiprois" and the "Chronicle of Amadi," with notes and introduction by J. L. LaMonte, and verse trans. by M. J. Hubert, N.Y. 1936.

Robert de Cléry (or Clari): *The Conquest of Constantinople* (La Conquête de Constantinople), English version from Old French by E. H. McNeal, N.Y. 1936; French ed. by Lauer, Paris 1924.

'Usāmah ibn Munqidh: *An Arab-Syrian Gentleman and Warrior in the Period of the Crusades: Memoirs of 'Usāmah ibn-Munqidh,* trans. from Arabic MS. by P. K. Hitti, N. Y. 1929.

Venette, J. F.: *The Chronicle of Jean de Venette,* English trans.

from Latin MS. in British Museum by Jean Birdsall, ed. with introduction and notes by Richard Newhall, N.Y. 1953.

William of Tyre: *A History of Deeds Done Beyond the Sea, by William, Archbishop of Tyre,* English trans. from Latin by E. A. Babcock and A. C. Krey, 2 vols., N.Y. 1943; text ed.: "Historia rerum in partibus transmarinis gestarum," in *Recueil, Historiens Occidentaux,* I (see above, section I); also 13th-century French version: *Guillaume de Tyr et ses continuateurs,* ed. by P. Paris, 2 vols., Paris 1879–80.

ADDITIONAL NOTES

A recent attempt in America to render into English some chronicles of the Crusades was made by Edward Noble Stone: *Three Old French Chronicles of the Crusades (University of Washington Publications in the Social Sciences,* X), Seattle, Wash., 1939.

The three chronicles are:

1. The History of the Holy War (L'Estoire de la Guerre Sainte), Being the Account of the Third Crusade, composed in verse by Ambrose, a jongleur in the service of Richard Lion-Heart about the year 1196. 1–160.

2. The History of Them that took Constantinople (Li estoires de Chiaus qui conquisent Constantinoble), Being an Account of the Fourth Crusade, which Robert of Clari in Amiénois. Knight, caused to be written down in the Picard tongue about the year 1216. 161–246.

3. The Chronicle of Rheims (La Chronique de Rains), Wherein is contained the History of the Emperors and Kings, Counts and Barons, Popes and Bishops who lived in France, Flanders, England, Germany, Italy and the Lands beyond the Sea, from the days of Lewis the Fat to those of Lewis the Saint, Written by an unknown Minstrel of Rheims in the year 1260. 249–357.

VII. BIBLIOTHECA GEOGRAPHORUM ARABICORUM

Ed. M. J. de Goeje, 8 volumes

A great project, begun under the general editorship of M. J. de Goeje in Holland, this contains a multitude of noteworthy Arab geographers from the earliest times. It has long served as the basic starting point in the study of Arab geography and the contributions of Arab geographers; though it is by no means a complete corpus of the material, which is spread widely throughout other projects and independent editions of the sources. An analysis of the contents of the *Bibliotheca* will be helpful to scholars of geography and cultural history.

Tome I (1st ed., Leiden 1870; 2nd ed. 1927).

Viae regnorum, descriptio ditionis Moslemicae, auctore Abu Ishāk al-Fārisī al-Istakhrī, ob. 951 A.D. (Al-Istakhrī: "Kitāb Masālik al-Mamālik"; based on al-Balkhī's work, "Ṣuwar al-Aqālīm," i.e., "Pictures of Regions.")

Tome II (1st ed., Leiden 1873; 2nd ed. 1938–39).

Viae et regna, descriptio ditionis Moslemicae, auctore Abu'l-Ḳāsim ibn Ḥaukal, ob. 977 A.D. (Ibn Ḥauqal: "Kitāb al-Masālik wa-l-Mamālik"; 2nd fuller edition by J. H. Kramers: *Opus geographicum, Kitāb Ṣūrat al-Arḍ*, 2 fasc., comprising Sijistan, Khurasan, and Transoxiania, with maps lithographed from original MSS.)

Tome III (1st ed., Leiden 1877; 2nd ed. 1906).

Descriptio imperii Moslemici, auctore Al-Mokaddasi, ob. 988 A.D. (Al-Maqdisi: "Kitāb Aḥsan al-Taqāsīm fī ma'rifat al-Aqālīm." Invaluable for historical geography, nomenclature, routes and commerce, local manners and customs, religious knowledge, accurate observation and general information on the places the author knew.)

Tome IV (Leiden 1879).

Indices, glossarium et addenda et emendenda ad part. I–III, auctore M. J. de Goeje.

Tome V (Leiden 1885).

Compendium libri "Kitāb al-Boldān," auctore Ibn al-Fakīh al-Hamadhānī, ob. post 903. (Abu Bakr ibn Muḥammed al-Hamadhānī, known as ibn al-Faqīh: "Kitāb al-Buldān," which is an indirect abridgment of a lost and more elaborate original.)

Tome VI (Leiden 1889).

Kitāb al-Masālik wa-l-Mamālik (liber viarum et regnorum), auctore Abu'l-Kāsim Obaidallah ibn Abdallah ibn Khordādhbeh (ob. 885 A.D.) et Excerpta e Kitāb al-Kharādj, auctore Kodāma ibn Dja'far. (Texts accompanied by translation into French; important for nomenclature, routes, commerce, finance, and administration. The second work of Qudāmah, d. post 932 A.D., consists of extracts from his treatise on taxation. Earlier translation by Barbier de Meynard. Cf. A Sprenger: *Die Post-und Reiserouten des Orients,* Leipzig 1864.)

Tome VII (2nd ed., Leiden 1892; 1st ed. by Juynboll, Leiden 1861).

Kitāb al-A'lak an-Nafīsa VII, auctore Abū Ali Ahmed ibn Omar ibn Rostah (ob. post 903 A.D.); et Kitāb al-Boldān, auctore Ahmed ibn abi jakub ibn Wadhih al-Katib al-Jakubi (ob. post 891 A.D.). (The first is the 7th volume of ibn Rustah's geographical encyclopedia; the second is al-Ya'quibi's well-known "Book of Countries." Earlier ed. by Juynboll, Leiden 1861; French trans. by G. Wiet, Cairo 1937.)

Volume VIII (Leiden 1894).

Kitāb at-Tanbīh wa-l-Ischrāf, auctore al-Masudi (ob. 956). Text, 2–401; Index and Glossary to Vols. VII and VIII, 402–508 and ix–xlii. (French trans. by B. Carra de Vaux: *Le Livre de l'avertissement et de la révision,* Paris 1896.)

ADDITIONAL NOTES

1. More material of the highest importance has been published in addition to the *Bibliotheca Geographorum Arabicorum* (see General Bibliography, section IV. 9). But the following additional selection is indispensable.

Dozy, R. and M. J. de Goeje (eds.) : al-Idrīsi (d. 1166 A.D.), *Description de l'Afrique et de l'Espagne,* Leiden 1866. Also see J. Jaubert: *Géographie d'Idrisi,* 2 vols., Paris 1838–40.

Ferrand, G. (ed. and French trans.) : *Instructions nautiques et routiers arabes et portugais des XVe et XVIe Siècles,* 3 vols., Paris 1921–28; see Vol. I for Arabic text of the Arab mariner Ahmad ibn Majid, promoter of the mariners' compass.

———: *Voyage du marchand arabe Sulayman en Inde et en Chine* (851 A.D.), Paris 1922.

Gaudefroy-Demombynes, M. (French trans.) : ibn Faḍl-Allāh al-'Umari, *L'Afrique moins l'Égypte* ("Masālik al-Abṣār Fī Mamālik-al-Amṣār"), Paris 1927.

Gelzer, H.: *Studien zur byzantinischen Verwaltung Ägyptens (Leipziger historische Abhandlungen, XIII),* Leipzig 1909.

Goeje, M. J. de (ed.) : al-Balādhuri (d. 892 A.D.), *Liber expugnationis regionum,* Leiden 1866; English trans.: *Origins of the Islamic State,* Vol. I by P. Hitti, N.Y. 1916, and Vol. II by F. C. Murgotten, N.Y. 1924; German trans. by O. Reschner, 2 vols., Leipzig 1917–23.

———: *Travels of ibn Jubair* (d. 1217 A.D.) *(Gibb Memorial Series,* V), London 1907.

Grohmann, A.: *Studien zur historischen Geographie und Verwaltung des frühmittel-alterlichen Ägypten (Österreichische Akademie der Wissenschaften,* 2. Abhandlung.), Vienna 1959.

Guest, R.: "The Delta in the Middle Ages," *Journal of the Royal Asiatic Society,* 1912, 941 ff.

Huart, C. (ed. and French trans.) : al-Maqdisi (d. 966 A.D.), *Livre de la création et de l'histoire,* 6 vols., Paris 1899–1919.

Jwaideh, Wadie: *The Introductory Chapters of Jāqūt's Mu'jam al-Buldān*, trans. and annot., Leiden 1955.

LeStrange, G. and E. A. Nicholson (eds. and English trans.) : al-Bal<u>kh</u>i (d. 919 A.D.), *Figures of Climes* ("Ṣūrat al-Aqālīm"), Cambridge 1921.

Meynard, Barbier de, and Pavet de Courteille (eds. and French trans.) : al-Mas'ūdi (d. 56 A.D.), *Les Prairies d'or* ("Murūj al-<u>Dh</u>ahab"), 9 vols., Paris 1861–77.

Minorsky, V. (trans.) : *Houdoūd al-'Alām* (The Regions of the World, 372 A.H./982 A.D.), Oxford 1937; also in *Gibb Memorial Series*, N.S., XI.

Mzik, H. v. (ed.) : *Das Kitāb Ṣūrat al-Ard des Abu Ga'far Muḥammed ibn Mūsa al-Huwarizmi* (d. between 835 and 844 A.D.), Leipzig 1926.

Reinaud, J. T. and M. S. Guyard (French trans.) : *Géographie d'Aboul-feda* (d. 1331 A.D.). Cf. *Taqwīn al-Buldān*, 2 vols. in 3, Paris 1848–83; *Ibn Battūṭa's Travels* (1325–54 A.D.), ed. with French trans. by D. Defréméry and B. R. Sanguinetti, 4 vols., Paris 1853 ff; selection in English by H. A. R. Gibb: *Travels in Asia and Africa*, London 1929; and latest and fullest version in English by H. A. R. Gibb: *The Travels of Ibn Battuta* A.D. *1325–1354*, I, London 1958.

Sachau, E. (English trans.) : *Al-Birūni's India* ("Kitāb al-Hind," c. 1050 A.D.), London 1914.

Sacy, S. de: (French trans.) : *La Relation de l'Égypte de Abdallatif, savant de Bagdad* (d. 1231 A.D.), Paris 1810.

Schier, C. (ed.) : *Géographie d'Ismael Abou'l Feda*, Dresden 1846.

Slane, M. G. de (French trans.) : al-Bakri (d. 1094 A.D.), *La Description de l'Afrique septentrionale*, 2nd ed., Algiers 1913.

Wiet, G. (ed.) : al-Maqrīzi (d. 1442 A.D.), "<u>Kh</u>iṭaṭ," Cairo 1911 ff, in progress. (A systematic description of Egypt and its important cities containing many historical notices.)

Yākūt al-Rumi: *Kitāb mu'djam al-buldān*, ed. by Muḥammed Amin al-Hangi, 10 bde., Cairo 1906–07; F. Wüstenfeld (ed.) : *Jacut's geographisches Wörterbuch*, 6 bde., Leipzig 1866–73; new ed. of Arabic text is in progress, Beirut, 1955 ff. Cf. F. J. Heer: *Die historischen und geographischen Quellen in Jaqut's geographischem Wörterbuche*, Strasbourg 1898.

2. Lists containing unpublished geographical tracts and materials may also be found in C. Brockelmann: *Geschichte der arabischen Litteratur*, 2 vols., Weimar 1898–1902; 2nd ed., Leiden 1943–49; Supp., 3 vols., Leiden 1937–42. Consult the following references: I, 257–64; II, 161–65, 229–30, 332–33, 344, 473–77, 495, 516–17, 554–55, 616–17, 643.

3. Also see General Bibliography, below, section IV. 9.

General Bibliography

I. BIBLIOGRAPHY

1. Western

American Historical Association: *A Guide to Historical Literature,* ed. by G. M. Dutcher, H. R. Shipman, S. B. Fay, A. H. Shearer, and W. H. Allison, N.Y. 1931, reprinted 1949. (Dana C. Munro supplied the bibliography for "A History of Mohammedanism and Moslem Peoples," and Louis J. Paetow wrote the bibliography for "Medieval Times 500–1450.")

————: *Guide to Historical Literature,* ed. by G. F. Howe, G. C. Boyce, T. R. S. Broughton, H. F. Cline, S. B. Fay, M. Kraus, E. H. Pritchard, and B. C. Shafer, N.Y. 1961. (Successor to 1931 edition. Bernard Lewis wrote the bibliography for "The Muslim World.")

British Museum Catalogue of Printed Volumes, 1881–1900; reprinted by J. W. Edwards, 58 vols. and 10-vol. Supp., Ann Arbor, Mich., 1946; Supp. 1950.

Chevalier, C. U. J.: *Répertoire des sources historiques du moyen âge.* (a) Bio-bibliographie, 2 vols., Paris 1877–88; 2nd ed., 1905–07. (b) Topo-bibliographie, 2 vols., Paris 1894–1903.

Dessubré, M.: *Bibliographie de l'ordre des Templiers, imprimés et manuscrits,* Paris 1928.

Germon, L. de, and L. Polain: *Catalogue de la bibliothèque de feu M. le comte Riant,* 2 vols., Paris 1899. (Library acquired by Harvard University in 1899. The late Professor John L. LaMonte's library was also acquired by Harvard University before his death.)

Graesse, Johann Georg: *Trésor de Livres Rares et Précieux, ou Nouveau Dictionnaire Bibliographique,* 8 vols., Milan 1950. (Notices on rare books.)

Malclès, L.-N.: *Les Sources du Travail—Bibliographies Spécialisées,* 2 vols., Geneva and Lille, 1952. Vol. 1, Bibliographies générales. Vol. 2 (2 pts.), Bibliographies spécialisées: Sciences humaines. Vol. 3, Bibliographies spécialisées: Sciences exactes et techniques. (This is a major guide to reference material of all kinds. Coverage extends to encyclopedias, dictionaries, works of reference, manuals, histories, periodicals, and source collections. The general pattern is to consider material in chapter form, beginning with a survey and then listing material, with analysis of contents or annotations where necessary.)

Masson, M.: *Éléments d'une bibliographie française de la Syrie (Congrès français de la Syrie, III),* Paris 1919.

Mayer, H.: *Bibliographie zur Geschichte der Kreuzzüge,* Munich 1960. (Well indexed.)

Molinier, A.: *Les Sources de l'histoire de France des origines aux guerres d'Italie (1494),* 6 vols., Paris 1901–06.

Paetow, A. C.: *Guide to the Study of Medieval History* (Medieval Academy of America), rev. ed., N.Y. 1931. (Excellent but outdated; hereafter referred to as *Guide.*)

Potthast, A.: *Bibliotheca Historica Medii Aevi (375–1500 A.D.),* 2 vols., Berlin 1896.

Walford, A. J.: *Guide to Reference Material,* London 1959. (A librarian's guide to reference books and bibliographies, with emphasis on current material and on material published in Britain.)

2. Arabic and Oriental

Also see below, section IV. 7, especially Literature.

Babinger, F.: *Die Geschichtsschreiber der Osmanen und ihre Werke*, Leipzig 1927.

Baumstark, A.: *Geschichte der syrischen Literatur mit Ausschluss der christlich-palästinischen Texte*, Bonn 1922.

Brockelmann, C.: *Geschichte der arabischen Litteratur*, 2 vols., Weimar 1898–1902; 2nd ed., Leiden 1943–49; Supp., 3 vols., Leiden 1937–42. (Monumental and indispensable register of practically all known Arabic works, notably in manuscript, thus saving preliminary labor in the innumerable catalogues of depositories and libraries throughout the world.)

Bursalī Mehmet Ṭahir: *Osmanlï Muellifleri* (Turkish), 3 vols., Istanbul 1333 A.H.

Chabot, J. B.: *La Littérature Syriaque*, Paris 1937.

Chauvin, V. C.: *Bibliographie des ouvrages arabes ou relatifs aux arabes, publiés dans l'Europe chrétienne de 1810 à 1885*, Liège and Leipzig 1892–1922.

Coult, L. H.: *An Annotated Bibliography of the Egyptian Fellah*, Miami, Fla., 1958.

Creswell, K. A. C.: *Bibliography of Arms and Armour in Islam*, London 1956.

————: "A Provisional Bibliography of the Muhammadan Architexture of India," *The Indian Antiquaries*, LI–1922 (May), 81–108.

Ettinghausen, R. (ed.) : *A Selected and Annotated Bibliography of Books and Periodicals in Western Languages dealing with the Near and Middle East* (Middle East Institute), 2nd ed. with Supp., Washington, D.C., 1954.

Gabriele, G.: *Manuale di bibliografia musulmana*, Rome 1916. (Incomplete but still useful.)

Gabrieli, Francesco: "Studi di storia musulmana, 1940–1950," *Revista Storica Italiana*, LII–1950, 99–111.

Golubovich, R. P. G.: *Biblioteca Bio-Bibliografica della Terra Santa e dell' Oriente Francescano*, series I, 9 vols., Florence 1906–27; series II, 14 vols., Florence 1921–39; series III, 2 vols., Florence 1928–48; series IV, ed. by M. Roncaglia, 2 vols., Cairo

1954. (Tremendous archival record of varied material, hereafter referred to as *Biblioteca*.)

Graf, G.: *Geschichte der christlichen arabischen Literatur*, 5 vols., Vatican City 1944–53.

Hill, R. W.: *A Bibliography of Libya*, Durham, N.C., 1959.

Kammerer, W. (with collaboration of S. M. Husselman and L. Shier): *A Coptic Bibliography*, Ann Arbor, Mich., 1950.

Karst, J.: *La Littérature géorgienne chrétienne*, Paris 1934.

Khalīfah, Hajji (Kātib Chelebi, d. 1658): *Kashf al-Dhunūn 'an Asāmi al-Kutub wa-l-Funūn* (The Clearing of Doubts Concerning the Titles of Books and Arts), 2 vols., Cairo 1858; also ed. by G. Flügel: *Lexicon Bibliographicum Encyclopedicum*, 7 vols., Leipzig and London 1835–58; reissued in Turkey under the auspices of the Ministry of Education, 2 vols., Istanbul 1941–43; continuation in 2 vols., Istanbul 1945–47. (Old but still useful; author used the immense manuscript treasures stored in Constantinople.)

Mantran, Robert: "Les Études historiques en Turquie de 1940 à 1945," *J.A.*, CCXXXV–1946–47, 89–111.

Mayer, Leo A.: *Bibliography of Moslem Numismatics, India Excepted*, 2nd ed., London 1954.

Minorsky, Vladimir F.: "Les Études historiques et géographiques sur la Perse," *Acta Orientala*, X–1932, 278–93; XVI–1937, 49–58; XXI–1951, 108–23.

Müller, A., *et al.*: *Orientalische Bibliographie*, Berlin 1887 ff.

Pearson, J. D.: *Index Islamicus 1906–1955* (School of Oriental and African Studies, University of London), Cambridge 1958. (A catalogue of articles in periodicals and other collective publications; detailed and excellent.)

Pfannmüller, D. G.: *Handbuch der Islam-Literatur*, Berlin and Leipzig 1923. (Describes European literature on Islam.)

Rizzitano, Umberto: "Studi di storia islamica in Egito (1940–1952)," *Oriente Moderno*, XXXIII–1953 (November), 442–56.

Rossi, Ettore: "Gli studi di storia ottomana in Europa, ed in Turchia nell ultimo venticinquennio (1900–1925)," *Oriente Moderno*, VI–1926 (August) 443–60. (Bibliography and critical survey of writings on Ottoman history.)

Salmaslian, A.: *Bibliographie de l'Arménie*, Paris 1946.

Sarkīs, Yūsuf Eliās: *Mu'jam al-Kutub al-'Arabiyah wa-l-Mu'arra-bah* (Dictionary of Arabic and Arabicized Books), Cairo 1928. (Lists all printed books in Arabic from the beginning of Arabic printing to 1919, with Supplements for publications after that date.)

Sauvaget, Jean: *Introduction à l'histoire de l'Orient musulman: éléments de bibliographie*, Paris 1946. (Survey of problems and sources of Islamic history, a large part of which is classified and annotated bibliography.)

al-Shayyāl, Gamāl al-Dīn: "A sketch of Arabic historical works published in Egypt and the Near East during the last five years (1940–1945)," *Royal Society of History Studies (Proceedings,* I), Cairo 1951, 143–74.

Spuler, B., and L. Forrer: *Der Vordere Orient im Islamischer Zeit (Wissenschaftliche Forschungsberichte, Geisteswissenschaftliche Reihe,* Hgb. K. Hon, Bd. 21, Orientalistik III), Bern 1954; new enlarged ed. by Claude Cahun in progress. (Especially valuable for Central Asia and the Volga basin.)

Storey, C. A.: *Persian Literature, A Bio-Bibliographical Survey,* 1 vol. in 3, London 1927–53. (List of Persian MSS. and printed works, with brief descriptions of them and their authors.)

Waxman, M.: *A History of Jewish Literature from the Close of the Bible Age to our own Days,* 4 vols., N.Y. 1938–47.

Wittek, Paul: "Neuere wissenschaftliche Literatur in osmanisch-Türkischer Sprache," *Orientalische Literaturzeitung,* XXXI–1928 (March), 172–76; XXXI–1928 (July), 556–62; XXXII–1926 (February), 74–79; XXXII–1926 (March), 244–50; XXXIV–1931 (May), 411–20.

Wright, W.: *A Short History of Syriac Literature,* London 1894.

II. CHRONOGRAPHY AND CHRONOLOGY

1. Western and Crusading

L'Art de Vérifier les Dates jusqu'à 1770, 4th ed. by Saint-Allais, 18 vols., Paris 1818–19.

Bond, J. J.: *Handy-Book of Rules and Tables for Verifying the Christian Era*, London 1889. (Cf. Paetow's *Guide*, 17 and 40 ff, for fuller resources.)

LaMonte, J. L.: "Chronologie de l'Orient Latin," *Bulletin de la Comité Internationale des Sciences Historiques*, XII–1943, pt. 2, 141–202.

Lane-Poole, R.: *Medieval Beckonings of Time*, London 1918.

Mas Latrie, L. de: *Trésor de chronologie, d'histoire et de géographie pour l'emploi des documents du moyen âge*, Paris 1889.

Philips, Cyril H. (ed.) : *Handbook of Oriental History*, London 1951. (Systems of transcription, names and titles, systems of dating, technical terms; also chronological and dynastic tables.)

Schlumberger, G., F. Chalandon, and A. Blanchet: *Sigillographie de l'Orient Latin*, Paris 1943. (Indispensable for Crusading chronology.)

Also see below, section IV. 1. W. B. Stevenson: *The Crusaders in the East*, Cambridge 1907, corrects much Crusading chronology (see General History), and H. Hagenmeyer has published research on the chronology of the First Crusade in the *Rev. Or. Lat.* (see First Crusade) .

2. Byzantine

Krumbacher, K.: *Geschichte der byzantinischen Literatur von Justinian bis zum Ende des oströmischen Reiches (527–1453)*, Munich 1897.

Muralt, E. von: *Essai de chronographie byzantine (1057–1453)*, Basle and Geneva 1871.

3. Arabic and Oriental

Berchem, M. van, and G. Wiet (eds.) : *Matériaux pour un Corpus Inscriptionum Arabicorum*, 7 vols., Cairo 1894–1930.

Caetani, L.: *Chronographia islamica*, 4 vols., Paris 1912–18. (Very detailed but incomplete, covering the period from the beginning of Islam in 622 to the end of the Umaiyad dynasty in 750 A.D./132 A.H.)

Cattenoz, H. G.: *Tables de concordance des ères chrétiennes et hégiriennes*, 2nd ed., Rabat 1954.

Edhem, H.: *Düwel-i-islamiye* (Turkish) , Istanbul 1927. (Based on Lane-Poole, amplified.)

Haig, Sir W.: *Comparative Tables of Muhammadan and Christian Dates*, London 1932. (Practical summary offering only the beginnings of years up to 2000 A.D.)

Lacoine, E.: *Table de concordance des dates des calendriers arabe, copte, géorgien, israélite, etc.*, Paris 1891.

Lane-Poole, S.: *The Mohammedan Dynasties*, London 1894; photographed ed., Paris 1925, containing synoptic tables giving Islamic and Christian years, together with summary historical notices.

al-Suwaidi, Muhammad Amin: *Sabā' ik al-Dhahab fī Ma'ri-fat Qabā'il al-'Arab*, Bagdad 1280 A.H. (Arabic genealogical tree from Adam to 19th century.)

Taqizadeh: "Various Eras and Calendars Used in the Countries of Islam," *Bulletin of the School of Oriental Studies*, IX–1938, 903–22 and X–1939, 107–32.

Wüstenfeld, H. F.: *Genealogische Tabellen der arabischen Stämme und Familien*, Göttingen 1852–53.

————: *Vergleichungs-Tabellen der mohammedanischen und christlichen Zeitrechnungen*, 2nd ed. by E. Mahler, Leipzig 1926. (Most detailed of all tables covering period to 1500 A.H. or 2076 A.D., with day-to-day reckonings, subject to error of one to three days resulting from difference of calculation between solar and lunar year reckonings.)

Zambaur, E. de: *Manuel de généalogie et de chronologie pour l'histoire de l'Islam: Textes, Tableaux et Cartes,* Hanover 1927. (Fullest attempt of its kind, arranged geographically and politically, with names completely transcribed, annotated, and documented; occasional errors to be corrected and lacunae to be filled, but this work is indispensable.)

III. HISTORICAL BACKGROUND

1. European History

Consult bibliographies in *Cambridge Mediaeval History,* ed. by J. B. Bury, 8 vols., Cambridge 1911–36. Other monumental sets published in many languages and many countries are enumerated in Paetow's *Guide,* rev. ed., N.Y. 1931. The *Shorter Cambridge Mediaeval History,* ed. by C. E. Prévité-Orton, 2 vols., Cambridge 1952, and other more recent studies, will be helpful in supplementing the older works and in bringing the student's bibliography up-to-date on the relevant points of European history. The *Histoire Littéraire de la France,* new ed., 36 vols., Paris 1865–1949, stands out as a work of exceptional value in the field (see above, Crusade Historiography).

2. Rome and Papacy

For detailed references to the Roman Church as a principal factor in the Crusade, see Paetow's *Guide,* rev. ed., N.Y. 1931.

CHIEF PRIMARY SOURCES

Acta Sanctorum, begun at Antwerp in 1643 and Venice in 1730; Paris ed. in 61 vols., 1863–83. (See *Analecta Bollandiana,* below.)

Analecta Bollandiana (Brussels, Société des Bollandistes), 78 vols., Paris 1882 to date (quarterly); gives current bibliography, with critical reviews of new publications, and supplements the *Acta* by printing texts, commentaries, etc., not included in the *Acta;* indices in 3 vols., T. I–XX (1882–91), XXI–XL (1902–22), XLI–LX (1923–42); later volumes individually indexed.

Annales Ecclesiastici (Baronius, Raynaldi, etc.), ed. by Mansi, 38 vols., Lucca 1738–59.

Eubel, C.: *Hierarchia catholica medii aevi sive summorum pontificum, cardinalium, ecclesiarum antistitum series ab anno 1198 usque ad 1431 perducta,* 2nd ed., I and II (Middle Ages), Münster 1913–14.

Liber Pontificalis, ed. by L. Duchesne, Paris 1884–92.

Patrologia Graeca, ed. by J. Migne, 165 vols., Paris 1857–92.

Patrologia Latina, ed. by J. Migne, 221 vols. in 222, Paris 1844–1904.

Regesta Pontificum Romanorum. Cf. Kehr, Jaffe, Potthast, Loewenfeld, Kaltenbrunner, and Ewald for editions.

"Rerum et personarum quae in Actis Sanctorum Bollandianis obviae ad Orientem latinum spectant index analyticus," ed. by Ch. Kohler, *Rev. Or. Lat.,* V–1897, 460–561; also in Kohler, *Mélanges pour servir à l'histoire de l'Orient latin et des Croisades,* Paris 1900–06, 104–212.

Sacrorum Conciliorum nova et amplissima collectio, ed. by Mansi, 53 vols., Florence and Venice 1759–1927.

SECONDARY LITERATURE

The secondary literature on the Latin Church is vast. The following selection may be pursued further by consulting the fuller lists compiled in regular bibliographical works.

Creighton, M.: *A History of the Papacy from the Great Schism to the Sack of Rome,* 6 vols., London 1897.

Fleury, C.: *Histoire écclésiastique,* 20 vols., Paris 1836–37. (Old but useful.)

Fliche, A., and V. Martin (eds.): *Histoire de l'église depuis les origines jusqu'à nos jours,* 26 vols., Paris 1934 ff. (Vols. 8–13 cover period of the Crusades.)

Gregorovius, F.: *Geschichte der Stadt Rom im Mittelalter,* 5th ed., 8 vols., Stuttgart 1903 ff; English trans. by Annie Hamilton: *History of the City of Rome in the Middle Ages*, 8 vols. in 13, London 1894–1902.

Hefele, C. J. von: *Conciliengeschichte*, 2nd ed. with additional material by A. Knöpfler and J. Hergenrother, 9 vols., Freiburg 1873–90; English trans. by R. Clarke, 5 vols., Edinburgh 1871–96; French trans. by H. Leclerq, 12 vols., Paris 1907–52.

Hélyot, P.: *Histoire des ordres monastiques, religieux et militaires, et de congrégations séculaires*, 8 vols., Paris 1711–21.

Landon, E. H.: *Manual of Councils*, 2 vols., Edinburgh 1893. (Church councils.)

Latourette, K. S.: *A History of the Expansion of Christianity*, 7 vols., N.Y. 1937–45. (Vol. II covers 500–1500 A.D.)

Mann, W. E.: *The Lives of the Popes*, 15 vols. in 16, London 1917–19; cont. by L. Pastor: *Geschichte der Päpste seit dem Ausgang des Mittelalters;* English trans. by F. I. Antrobus and D. F. Kerr: *The History of the Popes from the Close of the Middle Ages*, 12 vols., St. Louis, Mo., 1898–1912.

McKilliam, A. E.: *A Chronicle of the Popes from St. Peter to Pius X*, London 1912.

Milman, H. H.: *History of Latin Christianity*, 6 vols., London 1854–55.

Montalambert, C. F. R. de: *Histoire des Moines d'Occident depuis S. Bénoît jusqu'à S. Bernard*, 7 vols., Paris 1860–77; English trans. by F. A. Gasquet: *The Monks of the West*, 6 vols., London 1896.

Montor, A. de: *Histoire des Souverains Pontifes Romains*, 8 vols., Paris 1847.

Mourret, F.: *Histoire Générale de l'Église*, 9 vols., Paris 1909–20.

Meander, J. A.: *Allgemeine Geschichte der christlichen Religion und Kirche*, 6 vols., Hamburg 1826–52; English trans. by J. Torrey: *General History of the Christian Religion and Church*, 9 vols., London 1847–55.

Robertson, J. C.: *History of the Christian Church* (*64–1517*), 8 vols., N.Y. 1874.

3. Byzantium and the Byzantine Church

Atiya, A. S.: *Crusade, Commerce and Culture*, Bloomington, Ind., 1962. (See Index.)

Bréhier, L.: *Le Monde byzantin,* 3 vols., Paris 1947.

———: *La Querelle des images,* Paris 1904.

———: *Le Schisme oriental du XIe siècle,* Paris 1899.

Chalandon, F.: *Essai sur le règne d'Alexis Ier Comnène (1081–1118),* Paris 1900.

———: *Jean II Comnène (1118–1143) et Manuel I Comnène (1143–1180),* Paris 1912.

Couret, A.: *La Palestine sous les empéreurs grecs,* Grenoble 1896.

———: *La Prise de Jérusalem par les Perses en 614,* Orléans 1896.

Diehl, C., and G. Marçais: *Le Monde oriental de 395 à 1081,* Paris 1936.

———, L. Oeconomo, R. Guillaud, and R. Grousset: *L'Europe oriental de 1081 à 1453,* Paris 1945.

Duchesne, L.: *The Churches Separated from Rome,* English trans. by A. H. Matthew, London 1907.

Dvornik, F.: *The Photian Schism, History and Legend,* Cambridge 1948.

Finlay, G.: *History of Greece from Its Conquest by the Romans to the Present Time,* ed. by H. F. Tozer, 7 vols., Oxford 1877. (To be consulted along with E. Gibbon: *History of the Decline and Fall of the Roman Empire,* ed. by J. B. Bury, 7 vols., London 1896–1900.)

Fischer, W.: *Studien zur byzantinischen Geschichte des elften Jahrhunderts,* Plauen 1883.

Gaudefroy-Demombynes, M., and S. Platonov: *Le Monde byzantin jusqu'aux croisades,* Paris 1931.

Grühn, A.: *Die byzantinische Politik zur Zeit der Kreuzzüge,* Berlin 1904.

Hergenröther, J.: *Photius, Patriarch von Constantinople,* 3 vols., Regensburg 1867–79.

Howard, C. B.: *The Schism between the Oriental and Western Churches,* London 1892.

Jorga, N.: *Histoire de la vie byzantine,* 3 vols., Bucharest 1934.

Jugie, M.: *Le Schisme byzantin,* Paris 1941.

Laurent, J.: *Byzance et les turcs seldjoucides jusqu'en 1081,* Nancy 1913.

Miller, W.: "The Last Athenian Historian—Laonikos Chalkokondylas," *The Journal of Hellenic Studies,* XLII–1922, 36–49.

Millingen, A. van: *Byzantine Constantinople,* London 1899.

Neumann, C.: *Die Weltstellung des byzantinischen Reiches vor den Kreuzzügen* (Dissert.), Leipzig 1894; re-edited in French by Renauld and Kozlowski, with a foreword by Ch. Diehl, *Rev. Or. Lat.,* X–1903–04, 57–171; also published separately, Paris 1905.

Norden, W.: *Das Papsttum und Byzanz,* Berlin 1903.

Ostrogorsky, G.: *Geschichte des byzantinischen Staates,* Munich 1940; English trans. by Joan Hussey: *History of the Byzantine State,* Oxford 1956.

Pernice, A.: *L'Imperatore Eraclio,* Florence 1905.

Pichler, A.: *Geschichte der kirchlichen Trennung zwischen Orient und Okzident,* 2 vols., Munich 1864–65.

Schlumberger, G.: *Un Empéreur byzantin, Nicéphore Phocas,* Paris 1890.

——: *L'Épopée byzantine,* 3 vols., Paris 1896–1905.

——: *Récits de Byzance et des croisades,* 2 vols., Paris 1917–22.

Sherrard, P.: *The Greek East and the Latin West, A Study in the Christian Tradition,* Oxford 1959.

Vasiliev, A.: *Byzantium and the Arabs* (Russian), 2 vols., St. Petersburg 1900–02; French trans. by H. Grégoire and E. M. Canard: *Byzance et les arabes (Corpus Bruxellense Historiae Byzantinae),* Brussels 1935.

——:*History of the Byzantine Empire (324–1453),* in 1 vol., Madison, Wisc., 1952. (Contains extensive bibliography on Byzantine history.)

4. The Mediterranean

Béraud-Villars: *Les Normands en Méditerranée,* Paris 1951.

Farrūkh, 'Omar A.: *Islam and the Arabs in the Eastern Mediterranean down to the Fall of the Umayyad Caliphate (750 A.D.)* (Arabic), Beirut 1958.

——: *Islam and the Arabs in the Western Mediterranean during the Age of the Viceroys of Moslem Spain (711–756 A.D.)* (Arabic), Beirut 1950.

Halphen, L.: "La Conquête de la Méditerranée par les européens au XIe et au XIIe siècles," in *Mélanges d'histoire offerts à Henri Pirenne,* I, Brussels 1926, 175–80.

Herre, P.: *Der Kampf um die Herrschaft im Mittelmeer,* Leipzig 1909.

Monfroni, C.: *Il Dominio del Mediterraneo durante il Medio Evo* (reprinted from the *Rivista Marittima*), Rome 1900.

Philippson, A.: *Das Mittelmeergebiet, seine geographische und kulturelle Eigenart*, Leipzig 1904.

5. Mohammedanism, Muslim Peoples, and Ottoman History

Much of this material is indispensable background for the Crusade movement—the Crusades themselves, and their economic, social, intellectual, and political consequences. It is, moreover, the intention of the author in grouping together materials encompassing so wide an area—from Muḥammad through the 16th century—to indicate his conception of the Crusade, a movement with roots in history prior to Urban's summons, and with consequences ensuing beyond the time of the fall of Acre in 1291. (Also see Monumental Collections, above, especially notes to section I thereof, and General Bibliography, section IV. 3.)

ENCYCLOPEDIAS AND WORKS OF REFERENCE

Caetani, Leone: *Annali dell' Islam,* 10 vols. in 12, Milan 1905–26.

Cambridge Mediaeval History, ed. by J. B. Bury, 8 vols., Cambridge 1911–56; see Vol. II, chs. 10–12, and Vol. IV, ch. 10. (Excellent brief survey of early Muslim history, with bibliography.)

The Encyclopaedia of Islam, ed. by Th. Houtsma *et al.,* 4 vols., Leiden and London 1913; Supp., 1933; a new rev. ed. is in progress, under editorship of J. H. Kramer, H. A. R. Gibb, and E. Lévi-Provençal, Leiden and London 1954 ff.

Herbélot, Barthélémy d': *Bibliothèque orientale: ou dictionnaire universal contenant tout ce qui fait connaître les peuples d'Orient,* 4 vols., The Hague 1777–79.

Hughes, Thomas P.: *A Dictionary of Islam: being a cyclopaedia of the doctrines, rites, ceremonies, and customs, together with the technical and theological terms of the Muhammadan religion,* 2nd ed., London 1896.

SECONDARY LITERATURE

Amari, Michele: *Storia dei Musulmani di Sicilia,* 2nd ed., 3 vols., Catania, Sicily, 1933–39. (Fully documented from all known sources.)

Ameer, Ali Syed: *Short history of the Saracens, being a concise account of the rise and decline of the Saracenic power and of the economic, social, and intellectual development of the Arab nation from the earliest times to the destruction of Bagdad and the expulsion of the Moors from Spain,* rev. ed., London 1921. (Written from the standpoint of an enthusiastic Muslim.)

———: *Spirit of Islam, a history of the evolution and ideals of Islam, with a life of the prophet,* 2nd rev. ed., London 1922. (Muslim point of view.)

André, Pierre: *L'Islam et les races,* 2 vols., Paris 1922. (Vol. I is a general survey, of little value; Vol. II discusses sects, schisms, and local movements which led to the formation of separate states.)

Arnold, Sir Thomas W.: "Der Islam in Kleinasien: neue Wege der Islamforschung," *Zeitschrift der deutschen Morgenländischen Gesellschaft,* N.S., I–1922, 126–52.

———: *Preaching of Islam, a History of the Propagation of the Muslim Faith,* 3rd ed., N.Y. and London 1935.

Brockelmann, Carl: *Geschichte der islamischen Völker und Staaten,* Munich and Berlin 1939; trans.: *History of the Islamic Peoples,* London 1949.

Butler, Alfred J.: *Arab Conquest of Egypt and the Last Thirty Years of the Roman Dominion,* Oxford 1902.

Cahen, Claude: "La Première pénétration turque en Asie-Mineure," *Byzantion,* XVIII–1946–48, 5–67. (Turkish invasion of Asia Minor in 11th century.)

Canard, Marius: *Histoire de la dynastie des Ḥamdanides de Jazīra et de Syrie,* Paris 1953. (Describes Syria and Mesopotamia in the 10th century; Muslim-Byzantine relations.)

Caudel, Maurice: "Les Premières invasions arabes dans l'Afrique du Nord, 21–100 Heg., 641–718 J.-C.," *J.A.,* 9th sér., reprinted, Paris 1900.

Cheira, M. A.: *La Lutte entre Arabes et Byzantins: la conquête et l'organisation des frontières aux VIIe et VIIIe siècles,* Alexandria 1947. (Based on Arabic sources.)

Diehl, Charles, and Georges Marçais: *Le Monde orientale de 395 à 1081 (Histoire générale: Histoire du Moyen Âge, III),* Paris 1944.

Dozy, Reinhart P. A.: *Histoire des musulmans d'Espagne,* 4 vols., Leiden 1861; English trans. and ed. by F. G. Stokes: *Spanish Islam, a History of the Moslems in Spain,* London 1913. (Vol. I describes the Arabian origins of Hispano-Islamic factions and sects; Vol. III carries the post-Caliphal period to 1110. Cf. the work of E. Lévi-Provençal, below.)

Edib, Halide: *Conflict of East and West in Turkey,* Lahore 1935.

Elliot, Henry M., and John Dowson: *The History of India as told by its own Historians: the Muhammadan Period,* I–IV, London 1867–72. (These volumes relate to the period c. 700–1450.)

Fisher, S. N.: *The Middle East, A History,* N.Y. 1959.

Gabrieli, F.: *Gli Arabi,* Florence 1957.

Gaudefroy-Demombynes, M.: *La Syrie à l'époque des Mameloukes d'après les auteurs Arabes, description géographique, économique, et administrative, précédée d'un introduction sur l'organisation gouvernementale,* Paris 1923.

———, and S. Platonov: *Le Monde musulman et byzantin jusqu'aux Croisades,* Paris 1931.

———: *Les Institutions musulmanes,* Paris 1946; English trans. by J. P. MacGregor: *Muslim Institutions,* London 1950.

Gautier, Emile F.: *Le Passé de l'Afrique du Nord: les siècles obscurs,* Paris 1937. (The process by which North Africa passed from Christianity to Islam.)

Gibb, H. A. R.: *The Arab Conquests in Central Asia,* London 1923. (First phase of Muslim rule in Central Asia.)

———, and H. Bowen: *Islamic Society and the West, A Study of the Impact of Western Civilization on Moslem Culture in the Near East,* Vol. I in 2 pts., London 1950–57.

Gibbon, E.: *Decline and Fall of the Holy Roman Empire,* ed. by J. B. Bury, 7 vols., London 1896–1901; see chs. 50–52, 57. (Brief but competent survey of early Muslim history, with bibliography; hereafter referred to as *Decline and Fall.*)

Gibbons, H. A.: *The Foundations of the Ottoman Empire (1300–1403)*, Oxford 1906.

Gilman, Arthur: *The Saracens from the Earliest Times to the Fall of Bagdad*, N.Y. 1887.

Goeje, M. J. de: *Mémoire de la conquête de la Syrie*, 2nd ed., Leiden 1900. (Arab conquest of Syria in 7th century.)

Gonzalez Palencia, A.: *Historia de la España musulmana*, 4th ed., Barcelona 1945. (Full bibliography.)

Gordlevskii, Vladimir A.: *Gosudarstvo Sel'dzhukidov Maloi Azii* (The Seljuk State in Asia Minor), Moscow and Leningrad 1941.

Habibullah, A. B. M.: *The Foundations of Muslim Rule in India*, Lahore 1945.

Halid, Halil: *The Crescent versus the Cross*, London 1907.

Hammer-Purgstall, Joseph von: *Geschichte des osmanischen Reiches*, 10 vols., Pesth 1827–35; French ed. and trans. by J. J. Hellert, 18 vols., Paris 1835–43. (Wealth of Turkish authorities.)

Hitti, P. K.: *History of Syria*, 2nd ed., London 1957.

———: *History of the Arabs*, 6th ed., London 1956.

———: *Lebanon in History*, London 1957.

———: *The Near East in History*, N.Y. 1960.

Hodivala, Shahpurshah: *Studies in Indo-Muslim History*, Bombay 1939.

Huart, Clement L.: *Histoire des Arabes*, 2 vols., Paris 1912–13.

Jorga, Nicholas: *Geschichte des osmanischen Reiches*, 5 vols., Gotha 1908–13. (Good on social and economic history.)

Kritzeck, James, and R. Baylor Winder (eds.): *The World of Islam: Studies in honour of Philip K. Hitti*, N.Y. 1960. (Contains "A Bibliography of Works by Philip K. Hitti," 10–37.)

Lammens, Henri: *Études sur le siècle des Omayyades*, Beirut 1930. (Religious bias but scholarly.)

———: *La Syrie, précis historique*, 2 vols., Beirut 1921.

———: *L'Islam: croyances et institutions*, Beirut 1926; English trans. by E. D. Ross, London 1926.

Lane-Poole, Stanley: *History of Egypt in the Middle Ages*, new ed., London 1952.

Langer, W. L., and R. P. Blake: "The Rise of the Ottoman

Turks and Its Historical Background," *A.H.R.*, no. 3–1942, 468–505.

LeStrange, Guy: *Baghdad during the Abbasid Caliphate, from Contemporary Arabic and Persian Sources*, reprinted, Oxford and N.Y. 1924. (Collection of contemporary descriptive accounts.)

Lévi-Provençal, Évariste: *Histoire de l'Espagne musulmane*, 3 vols., Paris 1950–53. (The Umayyad Caliphate of Cordoba to 1031 A.D.)

Lewis, Bernard: *The Arabs in History*, 4th ed., London 1958.

Lybyer, A. H.: *The Government of the Ottoman Empire in the Time of Suleiman the Magnificent*, Cambridge, Mass., 1913.

Marçais, Georges: *Les Arabes en Berbérie du XIe au XIVe siècle*, Paris 1913. (The Bedouin invasion.)

——: *La Berbérie musulmane et l'Orient au Moyen Âge*, Paris 1946. (History of North Africa from the Islamic conquest to the decline of the Almohads.)

Margoliouth, David S.: *Mohammed and the Rise of Islam*, N.Y. 1905.

Marriott, J. A. R.: *The Eastern Question*, 4th ed., Oxford 1940. (From Ottoman rise.)

Mez, Adam: *Die Renaissance des Islams*, Heidelberg 1922; English trans. by S. Khuda Bukhsh and D. S. Margoliouth, London 1937. (Major work on cultural history of medieval Islam.)

Minorsky, Vladimir F.: *La Domination des Dailamites*, Paris 1932. (Outline of period of Buyid rule.)

Muir, Sir William: *The Caliphate: its Rise, Decline, and Fall*, new rev. ed. by T. H. Weir, Edinburgh 1915.

Müller, August: *Der Islam im Morgen-und Abendland*, 2 vols., Berlin 1885–87. (A political history written mainly from secondary sources.)

O'Leary, De Lacy: *A Short History of the Fatimid Khalifate*, N.Y. and London 1923.

Piquet, Victor: *Les Civilisations de l'Afrique du Nord: Berbères, Arabes, Turcs*, 2nd ed., Paris 1917.

Prasad, Ishwari: *History of Medieval India from 647 A.D. to the Mughal Conquest*, Allahabad 1925.

Ribera, Julian (trans.) : *Historia de la conquista de España de Abenalcofïya el Cordobes*, Madrid 1926.

Sanchez-Albornoz, Claudio: *La España musulmana segun los autores islamicos y christianos medievales,* 2 vols., Buenos Aires 1946. (Uses Arabic and Spanish historians.)

Sarkar, Jadunath (ed.) : *The Muslim period (The History of Bengal,* II) , Dacca 1948. (Follows Muslim annals.)

Sell, Edward: *Faith of Islam,* rev. ed., London 1908.

Spandugino, Teodoro: *Commentari dell' origine de Principi Turchi,* Florence 1551; French ed. by C. Schéfer, Paris 1896. (One of best early accounts.)

Spuler, Bertold: *Geschichte der islamischen Länder,* 2 vols., Leiden and Cologne 1952–53; English trans. by F. R. C. Bagley: *The Muslim World, A Historical Survey* (pt. 1, "The Age of the Caliphs," and pt. 2, "The Mongol Period") , Leiden 1960.

————: *Iran in früh-islamischer Zeit: Politik, Kultur, Verwaltung und öffentliches Leben zwischen der arabischen und der seldschukischen Eroberung 633 bis 1055,* Wiesbaden 1952. (Political history of Persia.)

Stripling, G. W. F.: "The Ottoman Turks and the Arabs," *Illinois Studies in the Social Sciences,* XXVI–1942–no. 4.

Vasiliev, A.: *Byzance et les Arabes,* 3 vols., Brussels 1935–50.

Weil, Gustav: *Geschichte der Chalifen,* 5 vols., Stuttgart 1846–62. (The last volumes concern the Mamluks and are entitled "Geschichte des Abbasidenchalifats in Egypten"; they are still the most comprehensive account extant.)

Wellhausen, Julius: *Das arabische Reich und sein Sturz,* Berlin 1902; English trans. by Margaret G. Weir, Calcutta 1927. (Arabic history to the fall of the Umayyads, 750 A.D.)

————: *Skizzen und Vorarbeiten,* 6 vols., Berlin 1884–99. (Vols. IV and VI include studies on the Prophet, the conquests, and the early Caliphate.)

6. Near Eastern Christianity

Adeney, W. G.: *Greek and Eastern Churches,* Edinburgh 1908.

Assemani, J. S.: *Bibliotheca orientalis,* 4 vols., Rome 1719–28.

Attwater, D.: *The Christian Churches of the East,* 2 vols., Milwaukee, Wisc., 1947–49.

Badger, G. P.: *The Nestorians and Their Rituals,* 2 vols., London 1852.

Browne, L. E.: *The Eclipse of Christianity in Asia, from the Time of Muhammad to the 14th Century*, Cambridge 1933.

Butcher, E. L.: *Story of the Coptic Church of Egypt*, 2 vols., London 1897.

Cash, W. Wilson: *Christendom and Islam, Their Contacts and Cultures down the Centuries*, N.Y. 1937.

Chabot, J. B. *et al.* (eds.): *Corpus Scriptorum Christianorum Orientalium*, Paris 1903 ff. (Work resumed by R. Draguet in Louvain; comprises Arabic, Coptic, Georgian, Armenian, and Ethiopian texts. This should be used with the *Patr. Or.*, ed. by R. Graffin and N. Nau, 27 vols., Paris 1903–54.)

Charles-Roux, F.: *France et Chrétiens d'Orient*, Paris 1939.

De Clercq, C.: *Églises unies d'Orient*, Paris 1934.

Dib, P.: *L'Église maronite*, Paris 1930; T. I only: "Le moyen âge."

Doresse, J.: *Au pays de la Reine de Saba—L'Éthiopie antique et moderne*, Paris 1956; English trans. by Elsa Coult: *Ethiopia*, London and N.Y. 1959.

Etteldorf, R.: *The Catholic Church in the Middle East*, N.Y. 1959.

Fortescue, A.: *Lesser Eastern Churches*, London 1913.

———: *Orthodox Eastern Churches*, London 1911.

———: *The Uniate Eastern Churches*, ed. by G. D. Smith, London 1923.

Grousset, R.: *Histoire de l'Arménie jusqu'à 1081*, Paris 1946.

Hardy, E. R.: *Christian Egypt, Church and People*, N.Y. 1952.

Hasluck, F. W.: *Christianity and Islam under the Sultans*, 2 vols., Oxford 1929.

Janin, R.: *Les Églises orientales et les rites orientaux*, 3rd ed., Paris 1926.

———: *Les Églises séparées d'Orient*, Paris 1927.

Kidd, B. J.: *The Churches of Eastern Christendom, from 451 A.D. to the Present Time*, London 1927.

Laurent, J.: *L'Arménie entre Byzance et l'Islam*, Paris 1919.

Leroy, J.: *Moines et monastères du Proche Orient*, Paris 1958.

Lequien, H.: *Oriens Christianus*, 3 vols., Paris 1740.

Macaire, G.: *Histoire de l'église d'Alexandrie*, Cairo 1894.

Maspéro, J.: *Histoire des Patriarches d'Alexandrie (518–616)*, Paris 1923.

Neale, J. M.: *History of the Holy Eastern Church,* London 1847–96; "General Introduction," 2 vols.; "Patriarchate of Alexandria," 2 vols.

Ormanian, M.: *The Church of Armenia,* 2nd ed., London 1955.

Parkhurst, S.: *Ethiopia—A Cultural History,* London 1955.

Rondot, P.: *Les Chrétiens d'Orient,* Paris 1955.

Serverus, bishop of Ashmunein: "History of the Patriarchs of the Coptic Church of Alexandria," Arabic text and English trans. by B. Evetts, in *Patr. Or.,* 4 fasc., Paris 1907 ff; continued for the Society of Coptic Archaeology by A. S. Atiya, Y. Abd al-Massih, and O. H. E. Burmester, in 4 fasc., Cairo 1943–59.

Shedd, W. A.: *Islam and the Oriental Churches, Their Historical Relations,* Philadelphia 1904.

Tournebize, F.: *Histoire politique et religieuse de L'Arménie, depuis les origines jusqu'à la mort de leur dernier roi, l'an 1393,* Paris 1910.

Tritton, A. S.: *The Caliphs and their Non-Muslim Subjects, A Critical Study of the Covenant of 'Umar,* London 1930.

Vries, G. de: *Oriente cristiano ieri e oggi,* Rome 1950.

Woodward, E. L.: *Christianity and Nationalism in the Later Roman Empire,* London 1916.

Worrell, W. H.: *A Short Account of the Copts,* Ann Arbor, Mich., 1945.

IV. THE CRUSADE MOVEMENT

1. The Crusades and the Latin Orient

See above, section I. 1 and section III. 3 for complementary materials.

LARGER WORKS

Certain works should be consulted because they devote entire sections to the Crusade in general. *The Cambridge Mediaeval History,* IV, chs. 12–14, and V, chs. 6–9, contains extensive bibliographies valuable for early literature. E. Lavisse and A. Rambaud are authors of the *Histoire Générale du IV Siècle à nos Jours,* 12 vols., Paris 1893–1901; new ed. with revised bibliographies, Paris 1927 (see Vol. II, ch. 4; consult D. C. Munro and G. C. Sellery: *Medieval Civilization,* N.Y. and London 1904, 248–56, for an English translation). In addition, consult E. Lavisse: *Histoire de France,* 9 vols. in 17, Paris 1900–11; see Vol. II, pt. 2, 227–50. Also E. Gibbon: *Decline and Fall,* ed. by J. B. Bury, 7 vols., London 1896–1901 (numerous other editions exist); and T. Arnold and A. Guillaume (eds.): *The Legacy of Islam,* Oxford 1931, 40–77.

SPECIAL ENCYCLOPEDIAS AND DICTIONARIES

The Encyclopaedia of Islam, ed. by Th. Houtsma *et al.,* 4 vols., Leiden 1913, with Supp. 1933; 2nd ed. in progress, ed. by J. H. Kramers, H. A. R. Gibb, and E. Lévi-Provençal, Leiden and London 1945 ff. The *Catholic Encyclopaedia,* ed. by C. G. Herbermann *et al.,* 12 vols., illus., with Supp. and Yearbook, N.Y. 1951 ff. The *Encyclopedia of Religion and Ethics,* ed. by J. Hastings with assistance of J. A. Selbie *et al.,* 12 vols. and Index, N.Y. 1908–26. The *Dictionnaire d'archéologie chrétienne et de liturgie,* ed. by F. Cabrol and H. Leclercq, Paris 1907 ff. The last two are part of a greater project bearing the general title of *Encyclopédie des Sciences Religieuses,* the biggest of its kind in history. The project comprises three other dictionaries: (1) *Dictionnaire de théologie catholique,* ed. by A. Vacant and E. Mangenot, Paris 1909 ff; (2) *Dictionnaire de la Bible;* (3) *Dictionnaire du Droit Canonique.* Of more direct interest is the antiquated but still useful *Dictionnaire historique, géographique et biographique des croisades,* ed. by Abbé Migne (*Nouvelle Encyclopédie Théologique,* XVIII), Paris 1852.

GENERAL HISTORY

(Including the arts, ecclesiastical and juridical matters)

Alphandéry, P.: *La Chrétienté et l'idée de croisades,* Paris 1954.

Archer, T. A., and C. L. Kingsford: *The Crusades*, London 1894.

Atiya, A. S.: *Crusade, Commerce and Culture*, Bloomington, Ind., 1962.

———: *The Crusade in the Later Middle Ages*, London 1938.

———: *The Crusade of Nicopolis*, London 1934.

———: "The Crusades: old ideas and new conceptions," *Journal of World History*, II–1954–55, 469–75.

Baldwin, M. W.: "Ecclesiastical Developments in the 12th Century Crusaders' State of Tripolis," *C.H.R.*, XXII–1936, 149–71.

——— (ed.) : *The First Hundred Years* (Pennsylvania *History of the Crusades*, I) , Philadelphia 1955.

Barker, E.: *The Crusades*, London 1925; originally article in *Encyclopaedia Britannica;* also in *The Legacy of Islam*, ed. by T. Arnold and A. Guillaume, Oxford 1931, 40–77.

Belloc, H.: *The Crusades*, London 1937.

Bent, J. T.: "The Lords of Chios," *E.H.R.*, IV–1889, 467–80.

Bercovici, K.: *The Crusades*, N.Y. 1919.

Bon, A.: "Recherches sur la principauté d'Achaïe 1205–1430," in *Études médiévales offertes à A. Fliche*, Paris 1952, 7–21.

Bramhill, E.: "The Privileges of the Crusaders," *American Journal of Theology*, V–1902, 279 ff.

Bréhier, L.: *L'Église et l'Orient au moyen âge—Les Croisades*, 6th ed., Paris 1928.

Bridey, E.: *La Condition juridique des croisés, et le privilege de la Croix*, Paris 1900.

Buchon, J.: *Histoire des conquêtes et de l'établissement des français dans les états de l'ancienne Grèce*, Paris 1846.

———: *Recherches et matériaux pour servir à une histoire de la domination française dans les provinces démembrées de l'empire grec*, 2 pts. in 1 vol., Paris 1840.

———: *Recherches historiques sur la principauté française de Morée et ses hautes baronnies*, 2 vols., Paris 1845.

Bury, J. B.: "The Lombards and Venetians in Euboea, 1205–1470," *Journal of Hellenic Studies*, VII–1886, 309–52; VIII–1887, 194–213; IX–1888, 91–117.

Cahen, C.: "Indigènes et croisés—quelques môts à propos d'un médecin d'Amaury et de Saladin," *Syria*, XV–1934, 351–60.

———: *La Syrie du Nord à l'Époque des Croisades*, Paris 1940.

Calthrop, M.: *The Crusades*, London n.d.

Campbell, G.: *The Crusades*, London 1935.

Conder, C. R.: *The Latin Kingdom of Jerusalem*, London 1897.

Coulton, G. G.: *Crusades, Commerce and Adventure*, London 1930.

Cox, G. W.: *The Crusades*, N.Y. 1887.

Deschamps, P.: "La Sculpture française en Palestine et en Syrie à l'époque des croisades," *Mon. et Mém.* (Fondation Piot), XXX–1930, 91–118.

Diehl, Ch.: "Les Monuments de l'Orient Latin," *Rev. Or. Lat.*, V–1897, 293–310.

Dodu, G.: *Histoire des institutions monarchiques dans le royaume de Jérusalem*, Paris 1894.

Ducange, C.: *Les Familles d'Outremer*, ed. by E. G. Rey, Paris 1869.

————: *Histoire de l'Empire de Constantinople sous les empéreurs français*, 1st ed., Paris 1657; new ed. in 2 vols., Paris 1826.

Ebersolt, S.: *Orient et Occident, Recherches sur les Influences Byzantines et Orientales en France avant et pendant les Croisades*, Paris 1954.

Enlart, C.: *L'Art Gothique et la Renaissance en Chypre*, Paris 1899.

————: *Les Monuments des Croisés dans le Royaume de Jérusalem, Architecture religieuse et civile*, 2 vols. and 2 atlases, Paris 1925–28.

Gerland, E.: *Geschichte des lateinischen Kaiserreichs von Konstantinopel (Geschichte der Frankenherrschaft in Griechenland, II)*, Hamburg vor der Höhe 1905.

————: "Histoire de la noblesse crétoise au moyen âge—Ire partie," *Rev. Or. Lat.*, X–1903–04, 172–247; Documents, XI–1905–08, 7–144. (Complete with detailed indices and bibliography.)

Gottlob, A.: *Ablassentwicklung und Ablassinhalt im 11. Jahrhundert*, Stuttgart 1907.

————: *Kreuzablass und Almosenablass*, Stuttgart 1906.

Grousset, R.: *Bilan de l'Histoire*, Paris 1946; English trans. by A. and H. Temple Patterson: *The Sum of History*, Oxford 1951.

————: *Les Croisades*, Paris 1944.

————: *L'Empire du Levant—Histoire de la Question d'Orient au moyen âge*, Paris 1946.

Grousset, R.: *L'Épopée des croisades,* Paris 1939.

———: *Histoire des croisades et du royaume franc de Jérusalem,* 3 vols., Paris 1934–36. (Ends with the fall of Acre in 1291. Grousset takes the "standard" view that the Crusade movement ended with the 13th century.)

Hansen, J.: *Das Problem eines Kirchenstaates in Jerusalem* (Dissert.) , Luxembourg 1928.

Hayek, D.: *Le Droit franc en Syrie pendant les croisades,* Paris 1925.

Heyck, E.: *Die Kreuzzüge und das heilige Land* (*Monographien zur Geschichte,* III) , Bielefeld and Leipzig 1900. (Short account, well illustrated.)

Hopf, K.: *Geschichte Griechenlands vom beginne des Mittelalters bis auf unsere Zeit (395–1821),* 2 vols., Leipzig 1867–68.

———: *Les Giustiniani, Dynastes de Chios,* French trans. by E. A. Vlasto, Paris n.d.

Hotzelt, W.: *Kirchengeschichte Palästinas im Zeitalter der Kreuzzüge, Palästinas von der Urkirche bis zum Gegenwart,* 3 vols., Cologne 1940.

James, G. P. R.: *The History of Chivalry,* N.Y. 1838. (Old romantic account of the Crusades.)

Jorga, N.: *Brève histoire des croisades et de leurs fondations en Terre Sainte,* Paris 1924.

———: "Un Projet relatif à la conquête de Jérusalem (1609) ," *Rev. Or. Lat.,* II–1894, 183–89.

Keeling, A. C.: *The Nine Crusades of the Middle Ages,* London n.d. (Minor literary accounts.)

Kohler, Ch. (ed.) : "Chartes de l'abbaye de Notre Dame de la vallée de Josaphat en Terre-Sainte (1108–1291). Analyse et extraits," *Rev. Or. Lat.,* VII–1899, 108–222.

———: "Description de la Terre-Sainte par un franciscain anonyme (1463) ," *Rev. Or. Lat.,* XII–1909–11, 1–67.

———: "Deux projets de croisade en Terre-Sainte composés à la fin du XIIIe siècle et au début du XIVe," *Rev. Or. Lat.,* X–1903–04, 406–57.

———: "Documents chypriotes du début du XIVe siècle," *Rev. Or. Lat.,* XI–1905–08, 440–52.

———: "Histoire anonyme de Jérusalem (1099–1187) , composée

peut-être à la fin du XIIe siècle," *Rev. Or. Lat.*, V–1897, 213–53.

————: *Mélanges pour servir à l'histoire de l'Orient Latin et des croisades*, 2 fasc., Paris 1906.

Kügler, B.: *Geschichte der Kreuzzüge*, Berlin 1891.

————: "Peter der Eremite und Albert von Aachen," *H.Z.*, XLIV–1880 (Neue Folge VIII) , 22–46.

Lamb, H.: *The Crusades—The Flame of Islam*, N.Y. 1931. (The author's other volumes on "Ghengis Khan" and "Tamerlane" are also readable light literature with a considerable background of erudition and imagination.)

————: *The Crusades—Iron Men and Saints*, N.Y. 1930.

Lammens, H.: "Relations officielles entre la cour romaine et les sultans mamlouks d'Égypte," *Revue de l'Orient Chrétien*, VIII–1903, 101–10.

LaMonte, J. L.: "The Communal Movement in Syria in the 13th Century," in *Haskins Anniversary Essays*, Boston and N.Y. 1929, 117–32.

————: *Feudal Monarchy in the Latin Kingdom of Jerusalem* (M.A.A.) , Cambridge, Mass., 1932.

————: "The Lords of Caesarea in the Period of the Crusades," *Speculum*, XXII–1947, 145–61.

————: "The Lords of Le Puiset on the Crusades," *Speculum*, XVIII–1942, 100–18.

————: "The Lords of Sidon in the 12th and 13th Centuries," *Byzantion*, XVII–1944–45, 183–211.

————: "The Rise and Decline of the Frankish Seigneury in the Time of the Crusades," *Revue Historique Sud-Est Européen*, XV–1938, 301–20.

————: "The Significance of the Crusaders' States in Medieval History," *Byzantion*, XV–1940–41, 300–15.

————: "The Viscounts of Naplouse in the Twelfth Century," *Syria*, XIX–1938, 272–78.

Longnon, J.: *L'Empire Latin de Constantinople et la principauté de Morée*, Paris 1949.

————: *Les Français d'Outremer au moyen âge*, Paris 1929.

————: "Le Rattachement de la principauté de Morée au royaume de Sicile en 1267," *J.S.*, 1942, 134–43.

Ludlow, J. M.: *The Age of the Crusades*, N.Y. 1896.

Madaule, J.: *L'Appel de la Terre Sainte*, Paris 1941. (Small essay.)

Mailly, J. B.: *L'Esprit des croisades, ou histoire politique et militaire des guerres entreprises par les chrétiens contre les mahométans, pour le recouvrement de la Terre Sainte, pendant les XIe, XIIe et XIIIe siècles*, 4 vols., Amsterdam and Paris 1780. (Old school.)

Maimbourg, L.: *Histoire des croisades pour la délivrance de la Terre Sainte*, 2 vols., Paris 1675-76. (One of the earliest.)

Mas Latrie, L. de: "Les Patriarches latins d'Alexandrie," *Rev. Or. Lat.*, IV–1896, 1–11.

———: "Les Patriarches latins d'Antioche," *Rev. Or. Lat.*, II–1894, 192–205.

———: "Les Patriarches latins de Constantinople," *Rev. Or. Lat.*, III–1895, 433–56.

Michaud, J. F.: *Histoire des Croisades*, with introduction on Michaud's life by M. Poujoulat, 6th ed., 6 vols., Paris 1841; first published in 3 vols., Paris 1812-17; afterward in 7 vols., Paris 1824-29, when the last four vols., on the sources, formed the *Bibliothèque des Croisades* (see above, Monumental Collections, section V) ; other editions, enlarged by M. Huillard-Bréholles, 4 vols., Paris 1856 and 1874; English trans. by W. Robson, 3 vols., London 1852 ff.

Miller, W.: *Essays on the Latin Orient*, Cambridge 1921.

———: *The Latins in the Levant, A History of Frankish Greece (1204-1566)*, London 1908.

Mills, C.: *The History of the Crusades for the Recovery and Possession of the Holy Land*, 2 vols., Philadelphia 1828; one-vol. ed., 1844. (Old school writing with an attempt at the use of original sources.)

Mombert, J. I.: *A Short History of the Crusades*, N.Y. 1894. (Small old manual.)

Munro, D. C.: *The Kingdom of the Crusaders*, N.Y. 1935. (Appendix by A. C. Krey contains complete bibliography of Munro's writings on the Crusades, 205 ff.)

———: "The Western Attitude towards Islam during the Period of the Crusades," *Speculum*, VI–1931, 329–43.

———, H. Prutz, and Ch. Diehl: *Essays on the Crusades* (reprinted from *International Monthly*) , Burlington, Vt., 19.

Newhall, R. A.: *The Crusades,* N.Y. 1927. (Small but well organized essay.)

Nicholas, R.: *Geschichte der Vorrechte und des Einflusses Frankreichs in Syrien und in der Levante, von Beginne des Mittelalters bis zum Friedenvertrag von Paris 1802,* Bern 1917.

Nicholson, R. L.: *Jocelyn I Prince of Edessa,* Urbana, Ill., 1954.

Paetow, L. J. (ed.) : *The Crusades and Other Historical Essays, Presented to Dana C. Munro,* N.Y. 1928. (Hereafter referred to as *The Crusades.*)

Paulus, N.: *Geschichte des Ablassess im Mittelalter von Ursprung bis zur Mitte des XIV Jahrhundert,* 2 vols., Paderborn 1922–23.

Pennsylvania *History of the Crusades,* originally planned by J. L. LaMonte, and continued by K. M. Setton, Philadelphia 1955 ff. (See M. W. Baldwin for Vol. I, and R. L. Wolff for Vol. II.)

Prawer, J.: "Colonization Activities in the Latin Kingdom of Jerusalem," *Rev. Belge,* XXIX–1951, 1063–1118.

————: "Étude de quelques problèmes agraires et sociaux d'une seigneurie croisée du XIIIe siècle," *Byzantion,* XXII–1952, 5–61, and XXIII–1953, 143–70.

————: "Les Premiers temps de la féodalité dans le royaume latin de Jérusalem," *Revue d'Histoire du Droit,* XXII–1954, 401–24.

Preston, H. G.: *Rural Conditions in the Kingdom of Jerusalem during the 12th and 13th Centuries* (Dissert.) , Philadelphia 1903.

Proctor, M. G.: *History of the Crusades,* Philadelphia 1889.

Rcy, E. G.: *Les Colonies franques de Syrie aux XIIe et XIIIe siècles,* Paris 1883.

————: "Les Dignitaires de la Principauté d'Antioche—grands officiers et patriarches (XIe–XIIIe siècles) ," *Rev. Or. Lat.,* VIII–1900–01, 117–57.

————: "Résumé chronologique de l'histoire des princes d'Antioche," *Rev. Or. Lat.,* IV–1896, 321–407.

Riant, comte: *Étude sur l'histoire de l'Église de Bethléem,* 2 vols., Geneva and Paris 1889–96.

Richard, J.: *Le Comte de Tripoli sous la dynastie toulousaine, 1102–1187,* Paris 1945.

▁▁, J.: "Pairie d'Orient Latin, les quatre baronnies des ▁aumes de Jérusalem et de Chypre," *Revue Historique de Droit Français et Étranger*, XXVIII–1950, 67–88.

———: *Le Royaume Latin de Jérusalem*, with Preface by G. Grousset, Paris 1953.

Röhricht, R.: *Geschichte der Königreichs Jerusalem (1100–1291)*, Innsbruck 1898. (Monumental erudition—rather heavy reading.)

———: *Geschichte der Kreuzzüge im Umriss*, Innsbruck 1899.

———: "Syria Sacra—Entwurf einer Kirchengeschichte des mittelalterlichen Syriens 1095 bis 1291," *Zeitschrift des Deutschen Palästina-Vereins*, X–1887, 1–48.

Rozière, E. de: *Cartulaire de l'église du Saint-Sépulchre de Jérusalem*, Paris 1849.

Runciman, S.: *A History of the Crusades*, 3 vols., Cambridge 1951–54. (Most extensive account in English.)

Schlumberger, G.: *Rénaud de Châtillon, Prince d'Antioche, Seigneur de la Terre d'outre-Jourdain*, Paris 1898.

Schwerin, U.: *Die Aufrufe der Päpste zur Befreiung des Heiligen Landes von den Anfängen bis zum Ausgang Innocent III—Ein Beitrag zur Geschichte der Kurialen Kreuzzugspropaganda und der päpstlichen Epistolographie* (Dissert.), Berlin 1937.

Stevenson, W. B.: *The Crusaders in the East*, Cambridge 1907. (Utilizes Arabic sources and corrects much Crusading chronology.)

Thousellier, C.: "Hérésie et croisade au XIIe siècle," *Rev. Écc.*, XLIX–1954, 855–72.

Throop, P. A.: *Criticism of the Crusade—A Study of Public Opinion and the Crusade Propaganda*, Amsterdam 1940.

Villey, M.: *La Croisade—Essai sur la formation d'une théorie juridique*, Paris 1942.

Vismara, G.: "Impium foedus—La illecicita delle alleanze con gli infedeli nella Repubblica cristiana medioevale," *Studi giuridici Urbinati*, Milan 1950, 107–209.

Waas, A.: *Geschichte der Kreuzzüge*, 2 vols., Fribourg i.B. 1956.

———: "Religion, Politik und Kultur der Geschichte der Kreuzzüge," *Welt als Geschichte*, 1951, 225–48.

Wietrowski, P. M.: *Historia de bello sacro pro liberanda Terra Sancta*, 3 vols., Prague 1724. (Old school.)

Wilken, E.: *Geschichte der Kreuzzüge nach morgenländischen und abendländischen Berichten*, 7 vols. in 8, Leipzig 1807–32. (Early monumental and comprehensive study, parallel to Michaud, but more serious and harder reading.)

Wilmot-Buxton, E. M.: *The Story of the Crusades*, London 1924. (Popular history first published in 1910 and followed by numerous reprints.)

Wolff, R. W., and H. R. Hazard (eds.): *The Later Crusades* (Pennsylvania *History of the Crusades*, II), Philadelphia 1961.

BACKGROUND TO CRUSADES

Barthold, W. W.: "Charles the Great and Harūn al-Rashīd" (Russian), *Khristianski Vostock*, I–1912, 69–94.

————: "The Question of Franco-Muslim Relations" (Russian), *Khristianski Vostock*, III–1914, 263–96.

Bréhier, L.: "Charlemagne et la Palestine," *R.H.*, CLVII–1928, 277–91.

————: "Les Origines des rapports entre la France et la Syrie—Le protectorat de Charlemagne?," *Congrès Français de la Syrie à Marseille*, 1919–fasc. 2, 15–39.

Brooks, E. W.: "The Byzantines and Arabs in the Time of the Early Abbasids," *E.H.R.*, XV–1900, 728–47 and XVI–1901, 84–92.

————: "The Struggle with the Saracens (717–867)," *C.M.H.*, IV, 119–38.

Buckler, F. W.: *Harūnu'l-Rashīd and Charles the Great* (M.A.A.), Cambridge, Mass., 1931.

Bury, J. B.: *A History of the Eastern Roman Empire from the Fall of Irene to the Accession of Basil I (802–67)*, London 1912.

————: *A History of the Later Roman Empire from Arcadius to Irene (395–800)*, new ed., 2 vols., London 1923.

Dorr, R.: *De bellis Francorum cum Arabicus gestis usque ad obitum Karoli Magni*, Königsberg 1861.

Gaudefroy-Demombynes, M., and S. Platonov: *Le Monde musulman et byzantin jusqu'aux croisades* (Histoire du Monde, VII), Paris 1931.

Harnack, A.: *Die Beziehungen des frankisch-italienischen zu dem byzantinischen Reich unter der Regierung Karls des Grossen und der späteren Kaiser Karolingischen Stämmes,* Göttingen 1880.

Hartmann, M.: "Die Islamisch-Frankischen Stattsvertrage," *Zeitschrift für Politik,* XI–1918, 1–64.

Jacob, G.: *Arabische Berichte von Gesandten an germanische Fürstenhofe aus dem 9 und 10. Jahrhundert,* Berlin 1927.

Joranson, E.: "The Alleged Frankish Protectorate in Palestine," *A.H.R.,* XXXIII–1927, 241–61.

Keller, F.: "Der Einfall der Sarazenen in die Schweiz," *Mitteilungen der Antiquarischen Gesellschaft in Zurich,* XI–1856–57, 1–30.

Kleinclausz, A.: "La Légende du protectorat de Charlemagne sur la Terre Sainte," *Syria,* VII–1926, 211–33.

Lokys, G.: *Die Kämpfe der Araber mit den Karolingern bis zum Tode Ludwigs II,* Heidelberg 1906.

Lopez, R. S.: "Mohammed and Charlemagne: a revision," *Speculum,* XVIII–1943, 14–38.

Paris, G.: "La Chanson du pèlerinage de Charlemagne," *Romania,* XI–1880, 1–50.

Pirenne, H.: *Mohammed and Charlemagne,* English trans. by B. Miall, London and N.Y. 1939.

Raine, J.: *St. Cuthbert,* Durham 1828. (His pallium was embroidered with Kufic Arabic inscriptions.)

Reinaud, J. T.: *Invasions des Sarrazins en France,* Paris 1836.

Runciman, S.: "The Byzantine 'Protectorate' in the Holy Land," *Byzantion,* XVIII–1948, 207–15.

———: "Charlemagne and Palestine?," *E.H.R.,* L–1935, 606–19.

Vailhé, S.: "La Prise de Jérusalem par les Perses en 614," *Rev. Or. Lat.,* II–1897, 125–64; VI–1901, 643–49.

Vasiliev, A.: *Byzantium and the Arabs* (Russian), 2 vols., St. Petersburg 1900–02; French trans. by H. Grégoire and E. M. Canard: *Byzance et les arabes (Corpus Script.,* I), Brussels 1935.

———: *History of the Byzantine Empire,* in 1 vol., Madison, Wisc., 1952; see chs. 5–6.

———: "Karl Veliki i Kharoun-ar-Raschid" (Russian), *Vizantiĭskiĭ Vremennik,* XX–1914, 64–116.

———: "The Struggle with the Saracens (867–1057)," in *C.M.H.,* IV, 138–51.

Zotenberg, H. H.: *Invasions des Visigoths et des Arabes en France,* Toulouse 1876.

PILGRIMAGE

Baumstark, A.: *Abendländische Palästinerpilger des ersten Jahrhunderts und ihre Berichte,* Cologne 1906.

Boulting, W.: *Four Pilgrims* (Trubner Oriental Series), London n.d. (Contains the travels of Huen-Tsiang (627–43) to sacred land of Buddha; of Saewulf, an English pilgrim to Palestine (1102); of ibn Battuta (1304–77), greatest of Muslim travellers; and of Ludovico Varthema of Bologna, who lived at the end of the 15th century and was a renegade pilgrim to Mecca and the foremost Italian traveller in the Renaissance.)

Golubovich, R. P. G.: *Biblioteca.* (See above section I. 2.)

Heath, S.: *Pilgrim Life in the Middle Ages,* Boston and N.Y. 1912; rev. ed.: *In the Steps of the Pilgrims,* London and N.Y. 1911.

Joranson, E.: "The Great German Pilgrimage of 1064–65," in Paetow, *The Crusades,* N.Y. 1928, 3–43.

Kötting, B.: *Peregrinatio Religiosa,—Wallfahrten in der Antike und des Pilgerwesen in der alten Kirche,* Münster 1950.

Lalanne, L.: "Des Pèlerinages en Terre Sainte avant les croisades," *E. de C.,* 1845–6, 1 ff.

Riant, P.: *Expéditions et pèlerinages des scandinaves en Terre Sainte au temps de Croisades,* Paris 1865.

———: "Pièces relatives au passage à Venise de pèlerins de Terre Sainte," *Archives,* II, 237–49 (see above, Monumental Collections, section III).

Röhricht, R.: *Bibliotheca Geographica Palästina,* Berlin 1890.

———: *Deutsche Pilgerreisen nach dem Heiligen Lande,* new ed., Innsbruck 1900.

Roussel, R.: *Les Pèlerinages à travers les siècles,* Paris 1954.

Also see below, section IV. 9, and above, Monumental Collections, section II.

FIRST CRUSADE

(Including the Peasants' Crusade)

CHIEF PRIMARY SOURCES

These are included in the *Recueil des Historiens des Croisades,* analyzed above, Monumental Collections, section I, and supplemented with Additional Notes. See also Crusade Historiography, as well as other bibliographical materials in A. C. Krey's *First*

Crusade (see below), and in Grousset, Runciman, Röhricht, and the Pennsylvania *History of the Crusades* (see above, section IV. 1, General History).

OTHER SOURCES

Alphandéry, P.: "Les Citations bibliques chez les historiens de la Première Croisade," *R.H.R.*, XCIX–1929, 139–57.

Anderssohn, J. C.: *The Ancestry and Life of Godfrey of Bouillon*, Indiana University, Bloomington, Ind., 1947.

Archer, T. A.: "The Council of Clermont and the First Crusade," *Scottish Review*, XXVI–1895, 274–95.

Baldwin, M. W.: "Some Recent Interpretations of Pope Urban's Eastern Policy," *C.H.R.*, XXV–1940, 459–66.

Bréhier, L.: *Un Évêque du Puy à la Ire Croisade, Adhémar de Montueil*, Le Puy 1910.

Cartellieri, A.: *Der Vorrang des Papsttums zur Zeit der ersten Kreuzzüge*, Munich 1941.

Cate, J. L.: "A Gay Crusader," *Byzantion*, XVI–1942–43, 503–26.

Chalandon, F.: *Histoire de la Première Croisade jusqu'à l'élection de Godefroi de Bouillon*, Paris 1925.

Charanis, P.: "Byzantium, the West and the Origin of the First Crusade," *Byzantion*, XIX–1949, 17–36.

Crégut, G. R.: *Le Concile de Clermont et la première croisade*, Clermont 1895.

———: "Le Voyage d'Urbain II en France," *Annales du Midi*, XLIX–1937, 42–69.

Crozet, R.: "Le Voyage d'Urbain II et ses négociations avec le clergé de France, 1095–96," *R.H.*, CLXXIX–1937, 271–310.

David, C. W.: *Robert Curthose, Duke of Normandy*, Cambridge 1920.

Dom Ruinart: "Vita Urbani II," in *Patr. Lat.*, CLI.

Duncalf, F.: "The Peasants' Crusade," *A.H.R.*, XXVI–1921, 440–54.

———: "The Pope's Plan for the First Crusade," in Paetow, *The Crusades*, N.Y. 1938, 44–56.

Erdmann, C.: *Die Entstehung der Kreuzzugsgedanken*, Stuttgart 1935.

Fliche, A.: "La Papauté et les origines de la croisade," *R.H.E.*, XXXIV–1938, 765–75.

————: *La Réforme Grégorienne et la Reconquête chrétienne (1057–1123)* (*Histoire de l'Église*, VIII), Paris 1940.

————: *Saint Grégoire VII*, Paris 1920.

————: "Urbain II et la Ire croisade," *Revue Historique de l'Église de France*, XIII–1927, 289–306.

Gay, J.: *Les Papes du XIe siècle et la chrétienté*, Paris 1926.

Glaesener, H.: "Autour de la bataille d'Ascalon—1099," *Rev. Belge*, XXVII–1949, 112–30.

————: "D'Antioche à Tortose, histoire et légende," *Rev. Belge*, XXII–1943, 35–58.

————: "L'Escalade de la tour d'Antioche," *Revue du Moyen Âge Latin*, II–1946, 139–48.

————: "Godefroid de Bouillon, était-il un médiocre?" *R.H.E.* XXXIX–1943, 309–41.

Goodsell, D. A.: *Peter the Hermit—A Story of Enthusiasm*, Cincinnati, O., and N.Y. 1906.

Hagenmeyer, H.: "Chronologie de la Première Croisade (1094–1100) ," *Rev. Or. Lat.*, VI–1898, 214–393, 490–549; VII–1899, 275–339, 430–503; VIII–1900–01, 318–82; reprinted, Paris 1902; continued as "Chronologie du royaume de Jérusalem," *Rev. Or. Lat.*, IX–XII–1902–09–11.

————: *Peter der Ermite, ein kritischer Beitrag zur Geschichte des ersten Kreuzzüges*, Leipzig 1879; French trans. by Furcy Reinaud: *Le Vrai et le faux sur Pierre l'Hermite*, Paris 1883.

Hill, J. H.: "Raymond of St. Gilles in Urban's Plan of Greek and Latin Friendship," *Speculum*, XXVI–1951, 265–76.

————, and Laurita L. Hill: "The Convention of Alexius Comnenus and Raymond of St. Gilles," *A.H.R.*, LVIII–1952–53, 322–27.

Holtzmann, W.: "Studien zur Orientpolitik des Reformpapsttums und zur Entstehung des ersten Kreuzzüges," *Historische Vierteljahrschrift*, XXII–1924, 167–99.

————: "Unionsverhandlungen zwischen Kaiser Alexios I und Papst Urban II im Jahre 1089," *Byzantinische Zeitschrift*, XXVI–1920, 38–67.

Klein, C.: *Raimund von Agulers—Quellenstudie zur Geschichte des ersten Kreuzzüges*, Berlin 1892.

Knappen, M. M.: "Robert II of Flanders in the First Crusade," in Paetow, *The Crusades*, N. Y. 1928, 79–100.

Krey, A. C.: *First Crusade: The Accounts of Eye-witnesses and Participants*, reprinted, Gloucester, Mass., 1958.

——: "Urban's Crusade, Success or Failure?" *A.H.R.*, LIII–1948, 235–50.

Kügler, B.: *Boemund und Tankred*, Tübingen 1862.

——: "Peter der Eremite und Albert von Aachen," *H.Z.*, XLIV–1880, 22–46.

Kuhne, E.: *Geschichte des Furstentums Antiochia unter normanischen Heerschaft (1098–1130)*, Berlin 1897.

Labaume, G. J.: *Adhémar de Monteuil, Évêque du Puy (1079–98)*, Le Puy 1910.

Le Febvre, Y.: *Pierre l'Ermite et la Croisade*, Amiens 1946.

Lobet, M.: *Godefroid de Bouillon*, Brussels 1943.

Manselli, R.: "Tancredi e Alessio Comneni a Constantinopoli e Pelekanon," *Archivio Storico per le provincie napoletane*, XXXIV–1955, 67–76.

Munro, D.C.: "Did the Emperor Alexis I ask for aid at the Council of Piacenza?" *A.H.R.*, XXVII–1922, 731–33.

——: "The Speech of Pope Urban II at Clermont," *A.H.R.*, XI–1906, 231–42.

Morghen, R.: *Gregorio VII*, Turin 1942.

Nicholson, R. L.: *Tancred—A Study of his Career and Work in Their Relation to the First Crusade and the Establishment of the Latin States in Syria and Palestine* (Dissert.), Chicago 1940.

Paulot, L.: *Un Pape français—Urbain II*, Paris 1903.

Pigeonneau, H.: *Le Cycle de la Croisade et la famille de Bouillon*, Saint Cloud 1877.

Porges, W.: "The Clergy, the Poor and the Non-Combatants on the First Crusade," *Speculum*, XXI–1946, 1–23.

Riant, P.: "Un Dernier Triomphe d'Urbain II," *R.Q.H.*, XXXIV–1883, 247–55.

Röhricht, R.: *Geschichte des ersten Kreuzzüges*, Innsbruck 1901.

Rousset, A.: *Les Origines et les Caractères de la Première Croisade* (Dissert.), Geneva and Neuchâtel 1945.

Runciman, S.: "Adhémar of Le Puy and the Eastern Churches," *Actes du VIe Congrès Internationale d'Études Byzantines*, II–1948, 318–32. (This should be read in conjunction with Vol. I of Runciman's *A History of the Crusades,* 3 vols., Cambridge 1951–54.)

———: "The First Crusader's Journey across the Balkan Peninsula," *Byzantion,* XIX–1949, 207–21.

———: "The Holy Lance Found at Antioch," *Analecta Bollandiana,* LXVIIII–1950, 197–209.

Sybel, H. von: *Geschichte des ersten Kreuzzugs,* 2nd ed., Leipzig 1881. (See also von Sybel's *History and Literature of the Crusades,* ed. and trans. by Lady Duff Gordon, London 1861. Pt. 1 is a translation of four lectures on the Crusades; pt. 2 is a translation from the preface to von Sybel's 1841 edition, and contains a criticism of the sources for the study of the First Crusade.)

Sydow, O. von: *Tancred—Ein Lebensbild aus den Zeiten der Kreuzzüge,* Leipzig 1880.

Thatcher, C. J.: "Latin Sources of the First Crusade," *Annual Report of the American Historical Association,* I–1900, 499–509.

Wolff, T.: *Die Bauernkreuzzüge des Jahres 1096, ein Beitrag zur Geschichte des ersten Kreuzzugs,* Tübingen 1891.

Yewdale, R. B.: *Bohemund I Prince of Antioch,* Princeton, N.J., 1924.

SECOND CRUSADE

CHIEF PRIMARY SOURCES

There are the Latin chroniclers, William of Tyre, Odo de Deuil, Otto of Freisingen, Helmold and Caffaro; the Greek chroniclers, John Cinnamus and Nicetas Choniates; and Armenian, Syriac, and Arabic chroniclers—Nerses Schnorhali, Matthew of Edessa, Michael the Syrian, Bar Hebraeus, Abu Shāmah, ibn al-Qālanisī, Usāmah, Kamāl al-Dīn, ibn al-Athīr and others.

Grumel, V.: "Au Seuil de la Deuxième Croisade, Deux lettres de Manuel Comnène au pape," *Revue d'Études Byzantines,* III–1945, 143–67.

James, Bruno Scott: *Letters of St. Bernhard of Clairvaux,* Chicago 1953.

Patr. Lat., T. 155, col. 1265–82: "Lettres des rois, princes et prélats de Terre Sainte au roi Louis VII."

Patr. Lat., T. 182–85: "Sancti Bernardi . . . Opera Omnia."

————, T. 185, col. 255 ff: "Sancti Bernardi Vita et res gestae."

Poole, R. L. (ed.) : *John of Salisbury—Historia Pontificalis*, Oxford 1927.

Suger de St. Denis: *Histoire du roi Louis VII*, ed. by A. Molinier, Paris 1887.

————: *Vie de Louis le Gros*, ed. by A. Molinier, Paris 1887; ed. by H. Waquet (*Les Classiques de l'Histoire de France au Moyen Âge*), Paris 1929.

OTHER SOURCES

Bernhardi, W.: *Konrad III*, Leipzig 1883. (Fullest account of German side.)

Caspar, E., and P. Rassow: "Die Kreuzzugsbullen Eugens III," *Neues Archiv*, XLV–1924, 285–305.

Constable, G.: "The Second Crusade as seen by Contemporaries," *Traditio*, IX–1935, 213–80.

Cosack, H.: "Konrads III. Entschluss zum Kreuzzug," *Mitteilungen des Instituts für oesterreichische Geschichtsforschung*, XXXV–1914, 278–96.

Délaruelle, Étienne: "L'Idée de croisade chez saint Bernard," in *Mélanges Saint Bernard*, Dijon 1954, 53–67.

Duval, R.: *Histoire politique, religieuse et littéraire d'Édesse*, Paris 1892.

Eales, S. J.: *The Life and Works of St. Bernard*, 3 vols., London 1889–96.

Gindler, P.: *Graf Baldwin I von Edessa*, Halle 1901.

Gleber, H.: *Papst Eugen III*, Jena 1936.

Hüffer, G.: "Die Anfänge des zweiten Kreuzzuges," *Historisches Jahrbuch*, VIII–1887, 391–429.

Kügler, B.: *Analekten zur Geschichte des zweiten Kreuzzuges*, Tübingen 1885.

————: *Neue Analekten*, Tübingen 1883.

Laurent, J.: "Des grecs aux croisés—Étude sur l'histoire d'Édesse entre 1071 et 1098," *Byzantion*, I–1924, 367–449.

Neumann, C.: *Bernhard von Clairvaux und die Anfange des zweiten Kreuzzuges*, Heidelberg 1882.

————: *Griechische Geschichtsschreiber und Geschichtsquellen in 12. Jahrhundert*, Leipzig 1882.

Pfeiffer, E.: "Beziehungen deutscher Cisterzienser und ihrer Klöster zu Kreuz-und Pilgerfahrten nach dem heilgen Lande zwischen dem zweiten und dritten Kreuzzug (1150–88)," *Cistercienser Chronik*, XLVII–1935.

Rassow, P.: "Die Kanzlei Bernhards von Clairvaux," *Studien und Mitteilungen zur Geschichte des Benediktinerordens und seiner Zweige*, N.S., III–1913.

Richard, J.: *Le comte de Tripoli sous la dynastie toulousaine (1102–1187)*, Paris 1945.

Séguin, A.: *Bernard et la Seconde Croisade* (Commission d'Histoire de l'Ordre de Citeaux), Citeaux 1953.

Vacandard, E.: "St. Bernard et la seconde croisade," *R.Q.H.*, XXXVIII–1885, 398–457.

———: *Vie de S. Bernard abbé de Clairvaux*, 2 vols., Paris 1895; see Vol. II.

Willems, E.: "Citeaux et la seconde croisade," *R.H.E.*, XLIX–1954, 116–151.

THIRD CRUSADE

CHIEF PRIMARY SOURCES

For a general outline of the sources of the Third Crusade, consult D. Bovée's dissertation (see above, Crusade Historiography listing).

The *Patrologia Latina*, ed. by J. Migne, 221 vols. in 222, Paris 1844–1904, contains letters from Christians in the East and papal letters of Gregory VIII (1187), Clement III (1187–91), and Celestine III (1198). See T. CCI, CCII, CCIV, and CCVI. T. CCVII, col. 1057–70, contains the work of P. de Blois: "De hierosolymitana peregrinatione acceleranda."

The most complete collection of English medieval chronicles is officially designated as *Rerum Britannicarum medii aevi scriptores, or Chronicles and Memorials of Great Britain and Ireland during the Middle Ages*, London 1858–1911, but popularly known as the *Rolls Series*, because it is published under the nominal direction of the Master of the Rolls, 99 vols. in 244, London 1858–96. For index to this series, see Gross, Charles: *Sources and Literature of English history from the earliest times to about 1485*, rev. 2nd ed., N.Y. 1915.

R. Howlett has edited the work of William of Newburgh:

"Historia rerum anglicarum," and its continuation to 1289, *Rolls,* 2 vols., London 1884–85; and also the work of Richard of Devizes: "De rebus gestis Ricardi Primi," *Rolls,* London 1886.

W. Stubbs has edited the "Itinerarium peregrinorum et gesta regis Ricardi," *Rolls,* London 1864; Benedict of Peterborough: "Gesta regis Henrici II et Ricardi I," *Rolls,* 2 vols., London 1867; Roger of Hoveden: "Chronica," *Rolls,* 4 vols., London 1868–71; and "De expugnatione Terrae Sanctae per Saladinum Libellus," *Rolls,* London 1875. The Curia Regis *Rolls* of the Reigns of Richard I and John have also been published, London 1922.

Extracts from the "Itinerarium Ricardi," and from Bohadin, Ernoul, Roger of Hoveden, Richard of Devizes, Rigord, ibn al-Athīr, Li Livres, Éracle, etc., have been selected and arranged by T. A. Archer: *The Crusade of Richard I (1189–92),* London 1900.

In *Monumenta Germaniae Historica* are to be found the following: the "Annales Marbacenses," XVII, 142–80; the "Chronica Slavorum" by Arnold of Lübeck, XXI, 101–250; the "Chronicon" by Burchard of Ursperg, XXIII, 333–83; the "Epistola de morte imperatoris," ss, 494–96: the "Chronicon, 1146–1209" by Otto of Saint Blaise, XX, 302–37; and the "Descriptio expeditionis Friderici I, 1189–90" by Tageno, dean of Padua, XVII, 509–17.

A. Chroust has edited the *Quellen zur Geschichte des Kreuzzuges Kaiser Friedrichs I,* N.S., V, Berlin 1928. Pt. 1 is the "Historia de expeditione Friderici imperatoris et quidam alii rerum gestarum fontes ejusdem expeditionis"; pt. 2 is the "Historia Peregrinorum, Expeditio asiatica Friderici I."

Also to be consulted are R. Röhricht: *Regesta Regni hierosolymitani (MXCVII–MCCXCI),* in 1 vol., Oeni Ponti, nos. 658 ff; P. Riant (ed.): *Haymar monachi: De expugnata* A.D. *MXCXI Accone liber tetrasticus,* Paris 1885; and J. Harttung: "Eine Kreuzzugsbulle Papst Gregors VIII," *Deutsche Geschichte,* XVII–1877, 620–22.

OTHER SOURCES

Baldwin, M. W.: *Raymond III of Tripolis and the Fall of Jerusalem (1140–1187),* Princeton, N.J., 1936.

Cartellieri, A.: *Philip II August König von Frankreich,* Leipzig 1906; see T. II: "Der Kreuzzug."

————: "Richard Loewenherz im heiligen Lande," *H.Z.*, CL–1908, 1–25.

Cazel, F. A.: "The Tax of 1185 in Aid of the Holy Land," *Speculum*, XXX–1955, 385–92.

Fischer, K.: *Geschichte des Kreuzzuges Kaiser Friedrichs I*, Leipzig 1870.

Flahiff, G. B.: "Deus non vult, A Critic of the Third Crusade," *Medieval Studies*, IX–1947, 162–68.

Gibb, H. A. R.: "The Arabic Sources of the Life of Saladin," *Speculum*, XXV–1950, 58–72.

Groh, F.: *Der Zusammenbruch des Reiches Jerusalem (1187–1189)*, Jena 1909.

Grühn, A.: *Der Kreuzzug Richards I*, Berlin 1892.

Lane-Poole, S.: *Saladin and the Fall of the Kingdom of Jerusalem*, new ed., London 1926.

Norgate, K.: *Richard the Lion Heart*, London and N.Y. 1924.

Prutz, H.: *Kaiser Friedrich I*, 3 vols., Danzig 1871–74.

Richard, J.: "An Account of the Battle of Ḥaṭṭīn Referring to the Frankish Mercenaries in Oriental Muslim States," *Speculum*, XXVII–1952, 168–77.

————: *Le Comte de Tripoli sous la dynastie Toulousaine (1102–1187)*, Paris 1945. (See above, Second Crusade.)

Riezler, S.: "Der Kreuzzug Kaiser Friedrichs I," *Deutsche Geschichte*, X–1870, 1–150.

Röhricht, A.: "Die Belagerung von Akka, 1189–91," *Deutsche Geschichte*, XVI–1876, 483–524.

————: "Die Rustungen des Abendlandes zur dritten grossen Kreuzzüge," *H.Z.*, XXXIV–1875, 1–73.

Schlumberger, G.: *Campagne du roy Amaury Ier en Égypte*, Paris 1906.

————: *Rénaud de Châtillon, prince d'Antioche*, Paris 1906.

Zerbi, P.: *Papato, impero e "Res publica Christiana" del 1187 al 1198*, Milan 1955.

HENRY VI'S PLAN OF CRUSADE

Leonhardt, W.: *Der Kreuzzugsplan Kaiser Heinrichs VI*, Leipzig 1913.

Torche, T.: *Kaiser Heinrich VI*, Leipzig 1867.

Traub, F.: *Der Kreuzzugsplan Kaiser Heinrichs VI in Zusammenhang mit der Politik des Jahre 1195–1197*, Jena 1910.

FOURTH CRUSADE

CHIEF PRIMARY SOURCES

These include *Sacrorum Conciliorum*, ed. by Mansi, 954–1086 and Supp. II, col. 861 ff.; *Patrologia Latina*, ed. by Migne, CCXIV–XV, containing Innocent III's "Epistolae" (1198–1207); Papal Epistles, ed. by Delisle, *E. de C.*, XXXIV–1873; and *Regesta Pontificum Romanorum*, ed. by Potthast, 2 vols., Berlin 1874–75. See also *Acta et Diplomata*, ed. by Miklosich and Müller, 6 vols., Vienna 1860–90. For the Venetian Archives, cf. G. L. F. Tafel and G. M. Thomas: *Urkunden zur altern Handels und Staatsgeschichte der Republik Venedig, Fontes Rerum Austriacarum, Diplomata et Acta*, XII–XIV, Vienna 1856–57; and Thomas and Tafel (eds.) : *Diplomatorum Veneto-Levantorum sive acta et diplomata res Venetas Graecas atque Levantis* (pts. 1 and 2 to 1454), in *Monumenti Storici publicati dalla R. Deputazione Veneta di Storia Patria*, seria prima, documenti, VIII and IX, Venice 1880–99.

See Monumental Collections, above, section VII, for Robert of Clari and for the *Exuviae* of Gunther of Paris. The most important eyewitness, however, is Geoffroy de Villehardouin: *La Conquête de Constantinople*, ed. by N. de Wailly, Paris 1872; new ed. by E. Faral, 2 vols., Paris 1938–39; earlier ed. by P. Paris, Paris 1838; early English trans. by T. Smith, London 1829; recent paperback edition by Sir Frank T. Marzials, N.Y. 1958.

OTHER SOURCES

Buchon, J. A. (ed.) : Ramon Muntaner, *Chronica o descripcio de la fets e hazanayes del inclyt rey Don Jaime*, French trans., 2 vols., Paris 1827; German trans. by K. F. W. Lanz, 2 vols., Leipzig 1842; English trans. by H. Goodenough: *The Chronicle of Muntaner* (H.S., series II), 2 vols., London 1920–21.

Cange, C. du: *Histoire de l'empire de Constantinople sous les empéreurs français*, Paris 1657; new ed. by J. A. Buchon, 2 vols., Paris 1826.

Cerone, F.: "Il Papa ed i Veneziani nella Quarta Crociata," *Archivio Veneto*, XXXVI–1888, 57–70 and 285–97.

Daru, P.: *Histoire de la république de Venise,* 4th ed., 9 vols., Paris 1853.

Diehl, C.: "The Byzantine Empire and the Crusades," in *Essays on the Crusades,* Burlington, Vt., 1903, 91–118.

———: "The Fourth Crusade and the Latin Empire," *C.M.H.,* IV–1923, reprinted 1936, 415–31.

Faral, E.: "Geoffroy de Villehardouin,—La question de sa sincérité," *R.H.,* CLXXVII–1936, 530–82.

Frolow, A.: "La déviation de la quatrième croisade vers Constantinople, Problème d'histoire et de doctrine," *R.H.R.,* CXLV, 68–87, and CXLVI, 67–89 and 194–219.

Gardner, A.: *The Lascarids of Nicaea, the Story of an Empire in Exile,* London 1912.

Gerland, E.: *Geschichte des lateinischen Kaiserreiches von Konstantinopel (Geschichte der Frankenherrschaft in Griechenland,* II), Hamburg vor der Höhe 1905; see pt. 1: "Geschichte der Kaiser Baldwin I und Heinrich (1204–1616)."

Grégoire, H.: "The Question of the Diversion of the Fourth Crusade," *Byzantion,* XV–1940–41, 158–66.

Gursch, M. R.: "A Twelfth Century Preacher—Fulk of Neuilly," in Paetow, *The Crusades,* N.Y. 1938, 183–206.

Halphen, L.: "Le rôle des 'Latins' dans l'histoire intérieure de Constantinople à la fin du XIIe siècle," in *Mélanges Ch. Diehl,* I, Paris 1930, 141–45.

Hodgson, F. C.: *Venice in the Thirteenth and Fourteenth Centuries,* London 1910.

Hopf, K. (ed.) : "Devastatio Constantinopolitana, Annales Harpipolenses," *M.G.H.,* ss, XVI, 9–12. Cf. *Chroniques Gréco-Romanes,* Berlin 1873, xiii–xiv and 86–92.

———: *Geschichte Griechlands vom Beginne des Mittelalters bis auf die neuere Zeit,* Leipzig 1867.

Hurter, F.: *Geschichte Papst Innocenz III und seiner Zeitgenossen,* 4 vols., Hamburg 1841–43; French trans. by A. de Saint-Chéron and J. B. Haiber, 3 vols., Paris 1855.

Janin, R.: "Au lendemain de la conquête de Constantinople, les tentatives d'union des églises—1204–14," *Échos d'Orient,* XXXII–1933, 5–21.

Longnan, J.: "Le Chroniqueur Henri de Valenciennes," *J.S.,* 1945, 134–50.

Longnan, J.: "Domination franque et civilisation grecque," in *Mélanges Ch. Picard*, II, Paris 1949, 659–67.

———: *L'Empire Latin de Constantinople et la Principauté de Morée*, Paris 1949.

——— (ed.) : *Histoire de l'Empéreur Henri de Constantinople*, Paris 1948. Cf. N. de Wailly (ed.) : Villehardouin, *La Conquête de Constantinople*, Paris 1872, 303–421.

——— (ed.) : *Livre de la Conquête de la Princée de l'Amorée, Chronique de Morée (1204–1305)*, Paris 1911.

———: "Problèmes de l'histoire de la principauté de Morée," *J.S.*, 1946, 73–93 and 147–61.

———: "Le Rattachement de la principauté de Morée au royaume de Sicile en 1267," *J.S.*, 1942, 134–43.

———: "Recherches sur la vie de Geoffroy de Villehardouin," *Hautes Études*, 1939–no. 276.

———: "Sur l'histoire de l'Empéreur Henri de Constantinople par H. de Valenciennes," *Romania*, LXIX–1946, 198–241.

Luchaire, A.: *Innocent III*, 6 vols., Paris 1905–08; see Vol. VI: "Question d'Orient."

Martini, G.: "Innocenzo III ed il finanziamento della Crociate," *Archivio della Società Romana di Storia Patria*, LXVII–1944, 309–35.

Mas Latrie, L. de (ed.) : *Chroniques d'Ernoul et de Bernard le trésorier*, Paris 1871.

———: *Les Princes de Morée ou d'Achaïe (1203–1461)*, Venice 1882.

Miller, W.: *Essays on the Latin Orient*, Cambridge 1921.

———: *The Latins in the Levant (1204–1566)*, London 1908.

Morel-Fatio, A. (ed.) : "Libro de los Fechos et Conquistas del Principado de la Morea, compilado per commandamiente de Don Fray Johan Fernández de Heredia, Mastre des Hospital de S. Johan de Jerusalem," published as the *Chronique de la Morée au XIIIe et XIVe siècles* (Soc. Or. Lat., Sér. Hist.), Geneva 1885.

Muralt, E. de: *Essai de Chronographie byzantine (1057–1453)*, 2 vols., Basle and Geneva 1871–73.

Muratori, L. A. (ed.) : *Rerum Italicarum Scriptorum*, new ed. by G. Carducci and V. Fiorini, Città del Castello 1900 ff; see T. XII: "Andrae Danduli Chronicon."

Norden, W.: *Der vierte Kreuzzug im Rahmen der Beziehungen des Abendlandes zu Byzanz*, Berlin 1898.

Papadopoulos-Kerameus, A.: "Documents grecs pour servir à l'histoire de la Quatrième Croisade (Liturgie et reliques)," *Rev. Or. Lat.*, VI–1898, 540–55.

Pauphilet, A.: "Robert de Clari et Villehardouin," in *Mélanges A. Jeanroy*, Paris 1928, 559–64. Cf. above, Monumental Collections, section VI.

———: "Sur Robert de Clari," *Romania*, LVII–1931, 289–311. Cf. above, Monumental Collections, section VI.

Pears, E.: *The Fall of Constantinople, Being the Story of the Fourth Crusade*, N.Y. 1886.

Riant, P.: "Le Changement de direction de la quatrième croisade," *R.Q.H.*, XXII–1878, 71–114.

———: "Innocent III, Philippe de Souabe et Boniface de Montferrat," *R.Q.H.*, XVII–1875, 321–75, and XVIII, 5–75.

Rodd, R.: *The Princes of Achaia and the Chronicles of the Morea, A Study of Greece in the Middle Ages*, London 1907.

Santifaller, L.: *Beiträge zur Geschichte des lateinischen Patriarchats von Konstantinopel (1204–61) und der venezianischen Urkunde (Historische-diplomatische Forschungen, Bd. 3)*, Weimar 1938.

Sathas, C. N.: *Bibliotheca Graeca Medii Aevi*, 7 vols., Venice and Paris 1872–94.

——— (ed.) : *Documents inédits relatifs à l'histoire de la Grèce au moyen âge*, 9 vols., Paris 1880–90.

Schlumberger, G.: *Byzance et Croisades*, Paris 1927.

Schmitt, J.: *Chronicle of the Morea*, London 1904.

Streit, L.: *Beiträge zur Geschichte des vierten Kreuzzuges*, Anklam 1877.

Tessier, J.: *La Quatrième Croisade—La Diversion sur Zara et Constantinople*, Paris 1884.

Thiriet, F.: "Les Chroniques vénitiennes de la Marcienne et leur importance pour l'histoire de la Romanie gréco-vénitienne," *Mélanges Archéologiques et Historiques*, LXVI–1954, 241–92.

Vasiliev, A.: "The Foundation of the Empire of Trebizond 1204–22," *Speculum*, X–1936, 1–37. Cf. Vasiliev: *History of the Byzantine Empire*, in 1 vol., Madison, Wisc., 1952.

Winkelmann, E.: *Philipp von Schwaben und Otto von Braun-schweig*, 2 vols., Leipzig 1873–78.

Wolff, R. L. : "Baldwin of Flanders and Hainault, First Latin Emperor of Constantinople—His Life, Death and Resurrection, 1172–1225," *Speculum*, XXVII–1952, 281–322.

———: "Mortgage and Redemption of an Emperor's Son, Castile and the Latin Empire of Constantinople," *Speculum*, XXIX–1954, 45–84.

———: "Romania—The Latin Empire of Constantinople," *Speculum*, XXIII–1948, 1–34.

Zaborov, A.: "La Papauté et la prise de Constantinople par les croisés," *Vizantiĭskiĭ Vremennik*, V–1952, 152–77.

———: "Les Préliminaires de la quatrième croisade," *Vizantiĭskiĭ Vremennik*, VI–1953, 223–35.

CHILDREN'S CRUSADE

Albertus Standensis: "Annales," ed. J. Lappenberg, *M.G.H.*, ss, XVI, 355. (Provides account of German participation.)

Alphandéry, P.: "Les Croisades d'enfants," *R.H.R.*, 1916, 73 and 259–82.

Gray, G. Z.: *The Children's Crusade—An Episode of the Thirteenth Century*, Boston and N.Y. 1898.

Hansberry, J. E.: "The Children's Crusade," *C.H.R.*, XXIV–1938, 30–38.

Janssens, G. de: *Étienne de Cloyes et les croisades d'enfants au XIIe siècle*, Paris 1891.

Munro, D.C.: "The Children's Crusade," *A.H.R.*, XIX–1914, 516–24.

Röhricht, R.: "Der Kinderkreuzzug, 1212," *H.Z.*, XXXVI–1876, 1–8.

Schwab, M.: *Les Croisades des Enfants*, Paris 1896.

FIFTH CRUSADE

CHIEF PRIMARY SOURCES

These include *Honorii III Romani Pontificis Opera Omnia*, ed. by C. A. Horoy, 5 vols., Paris 1879–82; *Regesta Honorii Papae III*, ed. by P. Pressutti, 2 vols., Rome 1888–95; and the Lives of St. Francis of Assisi in the *Acta Sanctorum*, 61 vols., Paris 1863–83. For the *Acta*, see *Analecta Bollandiana* (Brussels, Société des

Bollandistes), 78 vols., Paris 1882 to date (quarterly). The *Analecta* give the current bibliography of the subject and critical reviews of new publications, and supplements the *Acta* by printing texts, commentaries, etc., not inlcuded in the *Acta;* indices in T. I–XX (1882–91), XXI–XL (1902–22), XLI–LX (1923–42); later volumes are individually indexed.

For Arabic sources—e.g., ibn al-A<u>th</u>īr, Abul-Fīda, Abu Shāmah, ibn Wāṣil, and Maqrīsi—see above, Monumental Collections, section I, Additional Notes to part D.

OTHER SOURCES

Donovan, J. P.: *Pelagius and the Fifth Crusade,* Philadelphia 1950.

Hewlett, W. J. (ed.) : Roger of Wendover, "Flores Historiarum," 3 vols., *Rolls,* London 1886–89.

Greven, J.: "Frankreich und der fünfte Kreuzzug," *Historisches Jahrbuch,* XLIII–1923, 15–52.

Jacob of Vitry: "Historia Orientalis seu Hierosolymitana," in Bongars (ed.) , *Gesta,* I, 1047–1127; earlier ed., Douai 1597.

Meyer, P. (ed.) : "La Prise de Damiette en 1219, relation inédite en provençal," *E. de C.,* XXXVIII–1877, 496–571.

Michelant H., and G. Raynaud (eds.) : *La Dévise des chemins de Babiloine—Itinéraire à Jérusalem et descriptions de Terré Sainte* (Soc. Or. Lat., *Sér. géogr.*) , Geneva 1882.

Oliver von Paderborn: *Die Schriften des Kölner Domscholasters, späteren Bischofs von Paderborn und Kardinalbischofs von S. Sabina Oliverius,* ed. by H. Hoogeweg (*Bibliothek des Literarischen Vereins*) , Tübingen 1894; see pt. 1: "Historia Damiatina."

Röhricht, R.: "Briefe des Jacobus de Vitriaco, Bischofs von Accon, 1216–1221," *Zeitschrift für Kirchengeschichte,* XIV–1894, 97–117; XV–1895, 568–87; and XVI–1896, 72–114.

———: "Die Briefe des Kölner Scholasticus Oliver," *Westdeutsche Zeitschrift für Geschichte und Kunst,* X–1891, 161–208.

———: "Die Kreuzzugs bewegung im Jahre 1217," *Deutsche Geschichte,* XVI–1876, 137–58.

——— (ed.) : *Scriptores minores Quinte belli sacri* (Soc. Or. Lat., *Sér. Hist.,* II) , Geneva 1879. Comprises the following tracts: "Ordinacio de predicacione S. Crucis in Anglia"; "Gesta

Crucegerorum Rhenanorum"; "De itinere Frisonum"; "Gesta obsidionis Damiete"; John of Tulbia's "De domino Johanne rege Jerusalem"; "Liber duellii Christini in obsidione Damiate exacti"; "Fragmentum de captione Damiate provencialis textus cum versione gallica a Paulo Meyer confecta"; "Prophetiae cujusdam Arabicae in Latinorum castris ante Damiatam vulgatae verso quadruplex."

Röhricht, R.: *Studien zur Geschichte des fünften Kreuzzüges*, Innsbruck 1891.

———— (ed.) : *Testimonia minora de Quinto bello sacro* (Soc. Or. Lat., *Sér. Hist.*, III) , Geneva 1882.

Schwandtner, J. (ed.) : James Thwrocz, *Chronica Hungarorum* (*Scriptores Rerum Hungaricum*) , Vienna 1746.

Theiner, A. (ed.) : *Vetera Monumenta Historica Hungariam Sacram Illustrantia*, 2 vols., Rome 1859–60.

Thouzellier, Cr.: "La Légation en Lombardie du cardinal Hugolin (1221), Un épisode de la cinquième croisade," *R.H.E.*, XLV–1950, 508–42.

Van Ortroy, F.: "Saint François et son voyage in Orient," *Analecta Bollandiana*, XXXI–1912, 451–62.

SIXTH CRUSADE

CHIEF PRIMARY SOURCES

Also see Fifth Crusade, above.

Albéric or Aubry des Trois-Fontaines: "Chronica Alberici monachi Trium Fontium, a monacho novi monasterii Hoiensis interpolata," ed. by P. Scheffer-Boichorst, *M.G.H.*, ss, XXIII, 631–950.

Boehmer: *Regesta Imperii*, ed. by Picker, 5 vols., Innsbruck 1881–83.

Matthew of Paris: "Chronica majora," ed. by E. Luard, 7 vols., *Rolls,* London 1872–83.

Richardus de San Germano: "Chronica regni Siciliae," ed. by G. Pertz, *M.G.H.*, ss, XIX, 323–83.

Rodenberg (ed.) : *Epistolae saeculi XIII e regestis pontificorum selectae,* 3 vols., Berlin 1883–94.

Winkelmann, E. (ed.) : *Acta imperii inedita saeculi XIII,* 2 vols., Innsbruck 1880–85.

OTHER SOURCES

Blochet, E.: "Relations diplomatiques des Hohenstauffen avec les sultans d'Égypte," *R.H.*, LXXX–1902, 51–64.

Huillard-Bréholles, J. (ed.): *Historia diplomatica Friderici secundi*, 6 vols. in 12, Paris 1852–61.

Jacobs, W.: *Patriarch Gerold von Jerusalem, ein Beitrag zur Kreuzzugsgeschichte Friedrichs II*, Berlin 1872.

Kantorowicz, E.: *Frederick the Second*, London 1931.

Kestner, E.: *Der Kreuzzug Friedrichs II*, Göttingen 1873.

Knebel, W.: *Kaiser Friedrich II und Papst Honorius III in ihren gegenseitigen Beziehungen (1220–27)*, Münster 1905.

Reinaud, M.: "Histoire de la sixième croisade et de la prise de Damiette d'après les écrivains arabes," *J.A.*, VIII–1826, 18–40, 88–110 and 149–69.

Röhricht, R.: *Die Kreuzfahrt Friedrich II*, Berlin 1872.

Wiegler, P.: *The Infidel Emperor and his Struggle against the Pope, A Chronicle of the 13th Century*, English trans. by B. W. Downs, London 1930.

Winkelmann, E.: *Geschichte Kaiser Friedrichs des Zweiten und seiner Reihe*, Berlin 1863–65.

———: *Kaiser Friedrich II*, 2 vols., Leipzig 1889–97.

SEVENTH AND EIGHTH CRUSADES

CHIEF PRIMARY SOURCES

"Dépenses de Saint-Louis de MCCL à MCCLII," *R.H.G.F.*, XXI, 512–15.

Jean de Beaumont: "Lettre à Geoffroi de la Chapelle sur la prise de Damiette," *Archives*, I, 389–90 (see above, Monumental Collections, section III).

"Lettre de Guy de Mélun sur la prise de Damiette," in Michaud, *Bibliothèque*, IV, 611–19 (see above, Monumental Collections, section V).

"Lettre de Saint-Louis sur sa captivité et sa délivrance," in Michaud, *Bibliothèque*, IV, 619–31 (see above, Monumental Collections, section V).

"Ludovici regis de captione et liberatione sua epistola," in *Gesta*, ed. by Bongars, I (1196–1200), Hanover 1611.

Robert d'Artois: "Lettre sur la prise de Damiette," in Michaud,

Bibliothèque, IV, 610–11 (see above, Monumental Collections, section V) .

"Saint-Louis nolise seize navires génois pour sa première croisade," *Archives,* II, 232–36 (see above, Monumental Collections, section III) .

Sarrasin, Pierre Jean (Louis' chamberlain) : "Lettre à Nicolas Arrode, prévot des marchands de Paris en 1289 et 1291, sur la première croisade de Saint-Louis," in *Histoire et chronique du très chrétien roi Saint-Louis,* ed. by Michel, Paris 1881, 253–313.

OTHER SOURCES

For literary sources, Western and Eastern, see below, section IV. 2 and section IV. 7. Also consult Index.

Berger, E.: *Les Dernières Années de Saint Louis,* Paris 1902.

————: *Saint Louis et Innocent IV,* Paris 1893.

Davis, E. J.: *The Invasion of Egypt in* A.D. *1249 by Louis 9th of France,* London 1898.

Delaborde, H. F.: *Jean de Joinville et les seigneurs de Joinville,* Paris 1894.

Geoffroi de Beaulieu: "Vita et sancta conversatio piae memoriae Ludovici Noni regis Francorum," *R.H.G.F.,* XX, 1–27. (Written by order of Gregory X in 1272, after the author accompanied Louis in Egypt and Tunis.)

Guillaume de Chartres (Louis's chaplain) : "De vita et actibus inclytae recordationis regis Francorum Ludovici et de miracules quae ad ejus sanctitatis declarationem contigerunt," *R.H.G.F.,* XX, 27–41.

Guillaume de Nangis: "Chronicon 1226–1300," *R.H.G.F.,* XX, 543–82.

————: "Chronicon abrégée ou chronique des rois de France," *R.H.G.F.,* XX, 647–53.

————: "Gesta Ludovici regis," *R.H.G.F.,* XX, 312–465.

Guillaume de Saint-Pathus (Queen Marguerite's confessor) : *Les Miracles de Saint-Louis,* ed. by P. B. Fay, Paris 1931.

————: "Vie de Saint Louis," *R.H.G.F.,* XX, 58–121.

Guizot, M.: *St. Louis and Calvin,* London 1869.

Joinville, Jean de: *Histoire de Saint-Louis* (autobiography c. 1272–73) , ed. by N. de Wailly, Paris 1874; English trans. by J. Hutton, London 1868.

Jullien, P.: "Note sur l'emplacement de l'ancienne Damiette," *Bulletin de l'Institut Égyptien*, 2e sér., 1886–no. 6, 72–77.

Knox, W. F.: *The Court of a Saint*, London 1909.

Langlois, C. V.: *Saint Louis*, Paris 1886.

Lecoy de la Marche, A.: *France sous Saint-Louis et sous Philippe le Hardi*, Paris 1894.

Le Nain de Tillemont: *Vie de Saint-Louis*, 6 vols., Paris 1847–51.

Matthew of Paris: "Chronica Majora" and "Historia Minora," ed. by Madden, 3 vols., *Rolls*, London 1866–69.

Matthew of Westminster: "Flos Historiarum," ed. by Luard, 3 vols., *Rolls*, London 1890.

Norton, C. E.: *St. Louis and Joinville*, Boston 1864.

Paris, G. (ed.): "Jean de Joinville," in *Histoire Littéraire de France*, XXXII, Paris 1898, 291–459.

Perry, F.: *Saint Louis* (Heroes of Nations), N.Y. and London 1901.

Röhricht, R.: "Der Kreuzzug Louis IX gegen Damiette," *Kleine Studien zur Geschichte der Kreuzzüge*, Berlin 1890, 11–25.

——: "Der Kreuzzug Louis IX gegen Tunis," *Kleine Studien zur Geschichte der Kreuzzüge*, 25–28.

Sayous, A. E.: "Les Mandats de Saint Louis sur son trésor et le mouvement international des capitaux pendant la septième croisade, 1248–54," *R.H.*, 1931, 254–304.

Sepet, M.: *Saint Louis* (Les Saints), 7th ed., Paris 1905; English trans. by G. Tyrrell, London 1899.

Steinfeld, R.: *Ludwigs des heiligen Kreuzzug nach Tunis 1270 und die Politik Karls I von Sizilien*, Berlin 1896.

Wallon, H.: *Saint Louis et son Temps*, 4th ed., 2 vols., Paris 1895.

Walsh, vicomte: *Saint-Louis et son siècle*, Tours 1876.

2. The Crusade in the Later Middle Ages

PROPAGANDISTS AND MISSIONARIES

CHIEF PRIMARY SOURCES

For a wider perspective of the interesting propaganda literature in later medieval times, consult fuller analyses by Atiya: *The Crusade in the Later Middle Ages*, London 1938; Delaville LeRoulx: *La France en Orient au XIV siècle*, 2 vols., Paris 1886;

Golubovich: *Biblioteca* (see above, section I. 2); and Jorga: *Philippe de Mézières*, Paris 1896. Special work on the subject remains to be done, and much of the material, still in manuscript, awaits editors. A representative selection of the sources is given here for preliminary inquiry.

Adam, Guillaume d' (c. 1310): "De modo Sarracenos extirpandi," *Recueil, Documents arméniens,* II (see above, Monumental Collections, section I). Cf. *Rev. Or. Lat.,* X–1903–04, 16 ff.

Aeneas Silvius (Pope Pius II): *Opera.* See C. M. Ady: *Pius II,* London 1913, for editions.

Carmesson, J.: *Vita S. Petri Thomae, patriarchae Constantinopolitani, legati apostolici (Speculum Carmelitarum)*, ed. by Daniel de Sainte-Marie, Antwerp 1666.

Casola, Canon Pietro: *Pilgrimage to Jerusalem in the year 1494,* ed. by M. Margaret Newett, Manchester 1907.

Dubois, Pierre: *De recuperatione Terrae Sanctae,* ed. by V. Langlois (*Collection des textes pour servir à l'étude et à l'enseignement de l'histoire*), Paris 1891; English trans. by W. I. Brandt: *The Recovery of the Holy Land (Records),* N.Y. 1956 (see above, Monumental Collections, section VI).

Fidenzio di Padua: "Liber recuperatione Terrae Sanctae," in Golubovich, *Biblioteca,* II, Florence 1906–27, 9 ff.

Germain, Jean: "Le discours du voyage d'Oultremer au très victorieux roi Charles II prononcé en 1452," ed. by Schéfer, *Rev. Or. Lat.,* 1895-no. 2.

Lannoy, Ghillebert de (voyageur, diplomate et moraliste): *Oeuvres,* ed. by Potvin, Louvain 1878; English version: "Travels and Embassies," *Archaeologia,* XX–1821, 381–444.

L'Extrème Orient au moyen âge, d'après les mss. d'un Flamand de Belgique, moine de Saint-Bertin à Saint-Omer et d'un prince d'Arménie, moine de Prémontré à Paris, ed. by de Backer, Paris 1877.

Levanto, Galvano de (Philippe le Bel's physician, c. 1295): "De Recuperatione Terrae Sanctae," ed. by Ch. Kohler, *Rev. Or. Lat.,* VI–1898, 343 ff. (See also Vol. I of Levanto: *Mélanges pour servir à l'histoire de l'Orient Latin et des croisades,* 2 vols., Paris 1900–07.)

Lull, Ramon: *Opera Omnia,* ed. Salzinger, 8 vols., Mayence; new ed. from MSS. under direction of Salvador Galmes y Miguel Ferra: *Obrès*, 16 vols., Palma de Mallorea 1906–32.

Mézières, Philippe de: "Épistre lamentable et consolatoire," in Froissart, *Chroniques*, ed. by Kervyn de Lettenhove, XVI, Brussels 1872, 444–526.

————: "Militia Passionis Jhesu Christi," account of MSS. by Molinier, *Archives*, I, 335–64. (See above, Monumental Collections, section III.)

————: "Vita S. Petri Thomasii," *Acta Sanct.*, III, 605–11. (See above, section III. 2.)

Molay, Jacque de (Grand Maître du Temple): "Mémoire" (written c. 1307 on Crusade), in Étienne Baluze, *Vita paparum avenionensium*, ed. by Mollat, III, Paris 1914–27, 145 ff.; and in Delaville LeRoulx, *La France en Orient au XIVe Siècle*, II, Paris 1886, 3–6.

Nogaret, Guillaume de: "Mémoire sur la possibilité d'une croisade," in *Notes et extraits des* MSS. *de la Bibliothèque Impériale*, XX, Paris 1862, 199 ff.

Penna, Pietro de: "Libellus de locis ultramarinis," ed. by Ch. Kohler, *Rev. Or. Lat.*, IX–1902–nos. 3–4, 313–83.

Piloti, Emanuele: *De modo progressu ac diligenti providentia habendis in passagio Christianorum pro conquesta Terrae Sanctae tractatus*, ed. by Reiffenberg (*Collection des Chroniques Belges Inédits*, IV), Brussels 1846.

Recueil de Voyages et de documents pour servir à l'histoire de la géographie depuis le XIIIe jusqu'à la fin du XVIe siècle, publié sous la direction de Ch. Schéfer et Henri Cordier, 22 vols., Paris 1882–1908. (For annotation of the contents of this *Recueil*, see below, section IV. 9.)

Sanudo, Marino (Torsello, Il Vecchio): "Liber secretorum fidelium crucis super Terrae Sanctae recuperatione et conservatione," in Bongars (ed.), *Gesta*, II, Hanover 1611. Cf. English trans. of parts in *Palestine Pilgrims Text Society Library* (see above, Monumental Collections, section II).

Thaddeo of Naples: *Hystoria et desolacione et conculcacione civititatis Acconensis et Tocius Terre Sancte*, ed. by Riant, Geneva 1873.

Villamont, Jacques de: *Les Voyages du Seigneur de Villamont* [en Italie, Grèce, Terre-Sainte, Égypte et outres lieux] . . .

divisez en trois livres. . . plus un abrégé de la description de toute la France, reveu, corrigé, et augmenté de nouveau, Arras 1598. (For further editions, see below, section IV. 9.)

OTHER SOURCES

Ady, C. A.: *Pius II, the Humanist Pope,* London 1913.

Gottron, A.: *Ramon Lulls Kreuzzugsideen,* Berlin and Leipzig 1912.

Haureau, B. (ed.) : "Raimond Lulle," in *Histoire Littéraire de la France,* XXIX, Paris 1900, 1–386.

Haussler, M.: *Felix Fabri aus Ulm und sein Stellung zum geistigen Leben seiner Zeit,* Leipzig and Berlin 1914.

Hirsch-Gereuth, A. von: *Studien zur Geschichte der Kreuzzugsidee nach der Kreuzzügen,* Munich 1896.

Jorga, N.: *Philippe de Mézières (1327–1405) et la Croisade au XIVe Siècle,* Paris 1896.

Kampf, H.: *Pierre Dubois und die geistigen Grundlagen des französischen National-bewusstseins um 1300 (Beiträge zur Kulturgeschichte des Mittelalters und des Renaissance,* LIV), Berlin 1935.

Lemmens, L.: *Die Franziskaner im Heilige Lande,* 2nd ed., Münster 1925; see T. I: "Die Franziskaner auf dem Sion, 1335–1512."

Magnocavallo, A.: *Marino Sanudo il Vecchio e il suo Progetto di Crociata,* Bergamo 1901.

————: *Marino Sanudo il Vecchio e il Liber Secretorum fidelium crucis,* Milan 1898.

Parraud, A.: *Vie de S. Pierre de Thomas,* Avignon 1895.

Power, E.: "Pierre DuBois and the Domination of France," in *Social and Political Ideas,* ed. by F. J. C. Hearnshaw, London 1923, 139–66.

Powicke, E. M.: "Pierre DuBois," in *Historical Essays,* ed. by Tout and Tait, London 1902, 169–91.

Schucking, W.: *Die Organisation der Welt,* Leipzig 1909.

Vesnitch, R. M.: "Deux précurseurs français du pacifisme et de l'arbitrage internationale," *Revue d'Histoire Diplomatique,* XXV–1911, 23–78.

Zeck, E.: *Der Publizist Pierre DuBois, Seine litterarische Denk-*

und Arbeitsweise im Traktat "De recuperatione Terre Sancte," Berlin 1911.

THE LATER CRUSADE

CHIEF PRIMARY SOURCES

Sources are widely scattered in Western and Near Eastern chronicles and have been compiled in Atiya: *The Crusade in the Later Middle Ages,* London 1938, 541 ff.

Cabaret d'Orville, Jehan: *La Chronique du Bon Duc Leys de Bourbon,* ed. by A. M. Chazaud, Paris 1876.

Chalkokondylas, L.: "Historiarum de origine ac rebus gestis Turcarum" (Greek text and Latin trans.), in *Patr. Gr.,* CLIX; early French trans. by Blaise de Vigénaire: *Histoire de 1208 à 1483,* 2 vols., Paris 1662.

Cribellus, L.: "De Expeditione Pii Papae secundi in Turcas," in *Rerum Italicarum Scriptores,* ed. by L. A. Muratori, XXIII, Mediolani 1733, 21–80.

Ducas, Michael: *Historia Byzantina* (1341–1462), ed. by I. Bekker (*Corpus Script.*), Bonn 1834; also in *Patr. Gr.,* CXXXIX.

Froissart, Jean: *Chroniques,* ed. by Kervyn de Lettenhove, 25 vols., Brussels 1870–77. (Contains much additional material from the original sources in volumes of notes.)

Godefroy, T. (ed.): *Histoire de messire Jean de Boucicaut, mareschal de France, gouverneur de Gennes* (*Collection complète des Mémoires Relatifs à l'Histoire de France,* VI and VII), Paris 1825.

Golubovich, R. P. G.: *Biblioteca* (see above, section I. 2).

John VI Kantakuzenos (1320–57): *Historiae,* 3 vols., ed. by L. Schopen (*Corpus Script.*), Bonn 1828–32; also in *Patr. Gr.,* CII–IV.

Jorga, N.: *Notes et extraits pour servir à l'histoire des croisades au XVe siècle,* 6e sér., 6 vols., Paris and Bucharest 1899–1916.

——— (ed.): "Philippe de Mézières (1327–1405) et la croisade au XIVe siècle," *Hautes Études,* 1896–fasc. 110. (Thorough analytical study with extensive bibliography and valuable footnote references.)

Mas Latrie, M. de (ed.): "Commerce et expéditions militaires de la France et de Venise au moyen âge," *Doc. Inédits* (Mélanges historiques, III) , Paris 1835 ff.

Mas Latrie, M. de (ed.): Guillaume de Machaut, *La Prise d'Alexandrie* (Soc. Or. Lat.) , Geneva 1877.

Nicephoras Gregoras: *Historia Byzantina* (1204–1477) , 2 vols., ed. by I. Bekker (*Corpus Script.*) , Bonn 1829–35; also in *Patr. Gr.*, CXLVIII.

Pachymeres, George: *De Michaele Paleologe, De Andronico Palaeologo*, 2 vols., ed. by I. Bekker (*Corpus Script.*) , Bonn 1835; also in *Patr. Gr.*, CXLIII–IV.

Phrantzes, George: *Annales (1259–1477)* , ed. by I. Bekker (*Corpus Script.*) , Bonn 1838; also in *Patr. Gr.*, CXVI.

Schiltberger, I.: *Reisen des Johannes Schiltberger*, ed. by K. F. Neumann, Munich 1813; English trans. by J. B. Telfer, annotated by P. Brunn: *The Bondage and Travels of Johann Schiltberger* (H.S.) , London 1879.

Serviteur de Gui de Blois: "Relation de la croisade de Nicopoli," in Froissart, *Chroniques,* ed. by Kervyn de Lettenhove, XV and XVI, Brussels 1871.

OTHER SOURCES

Atiya, A. S.: *The Crusade in the Later Middle Ages,* London 1938.
———: *The Crusade of Nicopolis,* London 1934.

Boislisle, M. de: "Projet de croisade du premier duc de Bourbon," *Bullétin de la Société d'histoire de France,* 1872, 230–36 and 246–55.

Cahour, J.: *Les Dernières croisades et l'Europe musulmane au moyen âge,* Laval 1926.

Capitanovici, G. J.: *Die Eroberung von Alexandria,* Berlin 1894.

Chapman, C.: *Michel Paléologue, restaurateur de l'empire byzantin (1261–82)* , Brussels 1926.

Charrière, E.: *Négociations de la France dans le Levant (Doc. Inédits)* , 4 vols., Paris 1848–60. (Indispensable for the siege of Rhodes.)

Chevalier, U.: *La Croisade du dauphin Humbert II (1345–47)* , Paris 1920.

Courteille, Pavet de (trans. and ed.) : Kemal Pasha Zadeh (sheik-ul-Islam, 1525–33), *Histoire de la Campagne de Mo-*

hacs, Paris 1869. (Most important contemporary account of Mohacs campaign.)

Datta, P.: *Spedizione in Oriente di Amedeo VII conte di Savoia,* Turin 1826.

Delaville LeRoulx, J.: *La France en Orient au XIV siècle, Expéditions du maréchal Boucicaut,* 2 vols., Paris 1886.

Faure, C.: "Le Dauphin Humbert II à Venise et en Orient (1345–47)," *Mélanges d'Archéologie et d'Histoire* (École Française de Rome), XVII–1907, 509–62.

Gabotto, G.: *L'Età del conte verde in Piemonte, secondo nuovi documenti (1350–83),* Turin 1895.

Gay, J.: *Clement VI et les affaires d'Orient,* Paris 1904.

Gevay, Anton von: *Urkunden und Actenstücke zur Geschichte der Verhältnisse zwischen Österreich, Ungern und der Pforte im XVI. und XVII. Jahrhunderte,* Vienna 1840–42.

Halecki, O.: *The Crusade of Varna, A Discussion of Controversial Problems,* N.Y. 1943.

Heidelberger, F.: *Kreuzzugsversuche um die Wende des 13. Jahrhunderts,* Berlin and Leipzig 1912.

Herzsohn, I. J. P.: *Der Ueberfall Alexandrien's* (Dissert.), Bonn 1886.

Hintzen, J. D.: *De Kruistochts-plannen van Philips den Goede,* Rotterdam 1918.

Hopf, K.: *Les Giustiniani, dynastes de Chios,* French trans. by E. A. Vlasto, Paris 1888.

Jenkins, R. C.: *The Last Crusader, or the Life and Time of Cardinal Julian of the House of Cesarini,* London 1861.

————: "Un Projet relatif à la conquête de Jérusalem, 1609," *Rev. Or. Lat.,* II–1894, 183–89.

Jorga, N. (ed.): *Philippe de Mézières (1327–1405) et la croisade au XIVe siècle,* Paris 1896.

Kahle, P.: "Die Katastrophe des mittelalterlichen Alexandria," in *Mémoires de l'Institut de France,* LXVIII (Mélanges Maspero), pt. 3, Cairo 1935, 137–54.

Kupelweiser, L.: *Die Kämpfe Ungarns mit dem Osmanen bis zur Schlacht bei Mohacs (1526),* Vienna and Leipzig 1899.

Lecaille, H.: *Étude sur la Vie d'Enguerrand VII, sire de Coucy, comte de Soissons, 1340–97,* Mâcon 1890.

Loray, T. de: *Jean de Vienne, amiral de France, 1341–96,* Paris 1877.

Lot, H.: "Essai d'intervention de Charles le Bel en faveur des chrétiens d'Orient," *E. de C.,* 4e sér., XXXVI–1875, 588–600.

————: "Projets de croisade sous Charles le Bel et sous Philippe de Valois," *E. de C.,* 4e sér., V–1859, 503–09.

Manfroni, C.: *La Battaglia di Gallipoli e la politica venito-turca,* Venice 1902.

Mirot, L.: *Une Expédition française en Tunisie au XIVe siècle, le siège de Mahdia (1390),* Paris 1932.

Prutz, H.: *Rechnungen über Heinrich von Darbys Preussenfahrten (Verein für die Geschichte des Provinzen Ost-und Westpreussen),* Leipzig 1893.

Rosnak, Martin: *Die Belagerung der königliche Freystadt Guns,* Vienna 1789. (The Vienna campaign of Suleiman.)

Ursu, J.: *La Politique orientale de François Ier, 1515–47,* Paris 1908.

Zurlauben, baron de: "Abrégé de la vie d'Enguerrand VII du nom, sire de Couci, avec un détail de son expédition en Alsace et en Savoie," *Mon. et Mém.,* 1re sér., XXV.

MONGOLS AND MISSIONS

CHIEF PRIMARY SOURCES

Beazley, C. R. (ed.): *Texts and Versions of John de Plano Carpini and William de Rubruquis* (Latin and English, H.S., extra series), London 1903.

Bonaparte, Prince Roland (ed.): *Documents de l'époque mongole des XIIIe et XIVe siècles,* Paris 1896.

Dawson, C. (ed.): *The Mongol Mission—Narratives and Letters of the Franciscan Missionaries to Mongolia and China in the Thirteenth and Fourteenth Centuries,* trans. by a nun of Stanhope Abbey, N.Y. 1955. (Deals mainly with Plano Carpine and Rubruck.)

Golubovich, R. P. G.: *Biblioteca* (see above, section I. 2).

Hayton: *Histoire Orientale ou des Tartares, Recueil de divers voyages curieux faits en Tartarie, en Perse et ailleurs,* Leiden 1729.

Koehler, H. (ed.): *L'Église Chrétienne du Maroc et la Mission Franciscaine, 1220–1790,* Paris 1935.

Lull, Ramon: *Opera Omnia*, ed. by Salzinger, 8 vols., Mayence 1721–37; new ed. from MSS. under direction of Salvador Galmes y Miguel Ferra; *Obrès*, 16 vols., Palma de Mallorea 1906–32.

Ohsson, C. d': *Histoire des mongols, depuis Tchinguiz Khan jusqu'à Timour Bey ou Tamerlan*, 3rd ed., 4 vols., Amsterdam 1852.

Rachīd-ed-Dīn: *Histoire des Mongoles de la Perse*, ed. and French trans. by Quatremère, Paris 1836.

Rockhill, W. W. (ed.) : *The Journey of William Rubruk to Eastern Parts of the World, 1253–55, as Narrated by Himself, with Two Accounts of the Earlier Journey of Pian de Carpine* (H.S.) , London 1900.

Röhricht, R.: "Lettres de Ricoldo di Monte-Croce," *Archives*, II, 258–96. (See above, Monumental Collections, section III.)

OTHER SOURCES

Arnold, T. W.: *The Preaching of Islam*, 3rd ed. reproduced from 2nd, London 1935.

Batton, A.: *Wilhelm von Rübruck*, Münster 1921.

Barber, W. T. A.: *Raymond Lull—The Illuminated Doctor, A Study in Medieval Missions*, London 1903.

Barthold, W.: *Turkestan down to the Mongol Invasion*, trans. from Russian by H. A. R. Gibb, 2nd ed., London 1928.

Bouvat, L.: *L'Empire Mongol*, Paris 1927.

Browne, E. G.: *A Literary History of Persia*, 2nd ed., 4 vols., Cambridge 1929–30.

Browne, L. E.: *Eclipse of Christianity in Asia*, Cambridge 1933.

Cahun, L.: *Introduction à l'histoire de l'Asie, Turcs et Mongols dès origines à 1405*, Paris 1896.

Gindraux, J. A.: *Histoire du Christianisme dans le monde paien, les missions en Asie*, Geneva 1909.

Grousset, R.: *Conquérant du monde* (Jenghis) , Paris 1944.

———: *L'Empire des steppes*, Paris 1939.

———: *L'Empire mongol*, Paris 1941.

Hahn, H.: *Geschichte der Katholischen Missionen*, 5 vols., Cologne 1857–73.

Henrion, M. R. A.: *Histoire générale des missions catholiques depuis le XIIIe siècle*, 2 vols., Paris 1844–47.

Howorth, H. H.: *History of the Mongols from the 9th to the 19th*

Centuries, 4 vols., London 1876–80 and Vol. V with Indexes, 1927.

Hudson, G. F.: *Europe and China, Survey of their Relations from the Earliest Times*, London 1931.

Kulb, P. H.: *Geschichte des Missionsreisen nach den mongolei während des 13. und 14. Jahnhunderts*, Regensberg 1860.

Maclear, G. F.: *A History of Christian Missions during the Middle Ages*, 2nd ed., N.Y. and London 1904.

Marcellin de Civezza, R. P.: *Histoire Universelle des Missions Franciscaines*, trans. from Italian by R. P. Bernardin, Paris 1898.

Martod, H.: *Notes sur le Voyage de Fr. Jean de Plan-Carpin (1245–47)*, Paris 1912.

————: *Le Voyage de Fr. Guillaume de Rubrouck*, Couvin 1912.

Moule, A. C.: *Christians in China before the Year 1550*, London 1930.

Peers, E. A.: *Ramon Lull, A Biography*, London 1929.

Pelliot, P.: "Les Mongols et la Papauté—Documents nouveaux édités, traduites et commentés," *Revue de l'Orient Chrétien*, XXIII–1922–23, 3–30; XXIV–1924, 225–335; XXVIII–1932, 3–84.

Rémusat, Jean Pierre Abel: *Nouveaux Mélanges Asiatiques*, 2 vols., Paris 1828; see Vol. II, 199, for biographical material on Jean de Montecorvin (Giovanni di Monte Corvino or Montecroce).

Schlager, P.: *Mongolenfahrten der Franziskaner*, Trier 1911.

Yule, H.: *Cathay and the Way Thither, Being a Collection of Medieval Notices of China*, rev. ed. by H. Cordier, 3 vols. (H.S., ser. 2, Vols. 30, 37, and 38), London 1913–15.

Zwemer, S. M.: *Raymund Lull—First Missionary to the Moslems*, N.Y. 1902.

CYPRUS AND THE CRUSADE

CHIEF PRIMARY SOURCES

Amadi et Strambaldi: *Chroniques* (Italian), ed. by L. de Mas Latrie, 2 pts., Paris 1891–93.

Bustron, Florio: "Cronica, 1191–1489" (Italian), ed. by de Mas Latrie, *Doc. Inédits* (Mélanges historiques, V), Paris 1888,

1–532. Cf. *Bibliotheca Graeca Medii Aevi,* ed. by Sathas, II, Venice 1873.

Lusignan, P. Estienne de: *Description de Chypre,* Paris 1580.

————: *Généalogie des rois de Chypre,* Paris 1579.

Machaut, Guillaume: *La Prise d'Alexandrie* (Soc. Or. Lat.), ed. by L. de Mas Latrie, Geneva 1877.

Makhairas, Leontios: *Recital Concerning the Sweet Land of Cyprus Entitled "Chronicle,"* 2 vols., Greek text and English trans. by R. M. Dawkins, Oxford 1932; Greek text and French trans. by E. Miller and C. Sathas, 2 vols., Paris 1881–82; Greek text in *Bibliotheca Graeca Medii Aevi,* ed. by Sathas, II, Venice 1873.

Mas Latrie, L. de: *Documents génois concernant l'île de Chypre,* Paris 1894; also in *Archives,* II, pt. 2, 170–76 (see above, Monumental Collections section III).

————: "Documents nouveaux servant de preuves à l'histoire de l'île de Chypre sous le règne des princes de la maison de Lusignan," *Doc. Inédits* (Mélanges historiques, IV, Paris 1882), 337–99.

————: "Nouvelles preuves de l'histoire de Chypre," *E. de C.,* XXXII–1871, 341–78 and XXXIV, 47–87.

Raynaud, G.: "Gestes des Chyprois," *Recueil de chroniques françaises écrites en Orient aux XIIIe et XIVe siècles* (Soc. Or. Lat.), Paris 1887. Cf. *Recueil, Documents Arméniens,* II, 653–69 (see above, Monumental Collections, section I).

OTHER SOURCES

Alastos, D.: *Cyprus in History—A Survey of 5,000 years,* London 1955. (Extensive bibliography.)

Cobham, D. D.: *An Attempt at a Bibliography of Cyprus,* Nicosia 1929.

————: *Excerpta Cypria, Material for a History of Cyprus,* Cambridge 1908.

Dawkins, R. M.: *The Nature of the Cypriote Chronicle of Leontios Makhaires* (Lecture), Oxford 1945.

Enlart, E.: *L'Art gothique et la renaissance en Chypre,* 2 vols., Paris 1899.

Gunnis, R.: *Historic Cyprus,* London 1936.

Hackett, J.: *A History of the Orthodox Church of Cyprus,* London 1901.

Hill, G.: *History of Cyprus,* 3 vols., Cambridge 1948.

Hogarth, D. G.: *Devia Cypria,* London 1898.

Lang, R. H.: *Cyprus, Its History, Its Present Resources and Future Prospects,* London 1878.

Luke, H.: *Cyprus Under the Turks,* Oxford 1921.

Mallock, W. H.: *In an Enchanted Island,* London 1889.

Mariti, l'abbé: *Travels through Cyprus, Syria and Palestine with a General History of the Levant,* 2 vols., Dublin 1792.

Mas Latrie, L. de: "Archevêques Latins de l'île de Chypre," *Archives,* II, pt. 1, 207–328. (See above, Monumental Collections, section III.)

————: *Généalogie des Rois de Chypre de la famille de Lusignan* (extrait de *l'Archivio Veneta*), Venice 1881.

————: *Histoire de l'île de Chypre sous le règne des princes de la maison de Lusignan,* 3 vols., Paris 1855–61.

Stewart, B.: *Cyprus—The People, Mediaeval Cities, Castles, Antiquities, and History of the Island,* London 1908.

Storrs, R.: *A Chronology of Cyprus,* Nicosia 1930.

————: *The Handbook of Cyprus,* London 1930.

Stubbs, W.: "The Medieval Kingdoms of Cyprus and Armenia," ch. VIII in *Seventeen Lectures on the Study of Mediaeval and Modern History and Kindred Subjects,* 3rd ed., Oxford 1900.

3. Aftermath of the Crusades

Also see above, section III, especially pts. 3 and 5. For Armenia, see above, Monumental Collections, Notes to section I. For Cyprus, see above, section IV.2, Cyprus and the Crusade.

THE COUNTER-CRUSADE

CHIEF PRIMARY SOURCES

Eastern sources include al-Bukhārī (d. 870 A.D.) : *Les Traditions islamiques,* French trans. from Arabic with Notes and Index by O. Houdas and W. Marçais, 3 vols., Paris 1903–08; al-Qāḍi al-Nuʿmān (d. 974 A.D.) : *Kitāb al-Jihād wal-Muqaddamāt,* ed. by ʾAṣif ibn ʿAli Aṣghar Faiẓi, Cairo 1951; and ibn Taimiyya (d. 1328 A.D.) : *Ziyārāt al-Qubūr wal-Istinjād bil-Qubūr,* risāla (tract) no. 6 of Majmū'at al-Rasā'il, Cairo, 1317 A.H. For fuller list of books on Jihād, Visitation, and Virtues, see Atiya: *The Crusade in the Later Middle Ages,* London 1938.

OTHER SOURCES

Adams, C. C.: "Abū Ḥanīfah, Champion of Liberalism and Tolerance in Islam," *The Moslem World,* XXXVI–1946, 217–27.

Arnold, T. W.: *The Preaching of Islam,* 3rd ed., London 1935.

Bates, M. S.: "Islam and Religious Liberty," *The Moslem World,* XXXVI–1946, 54–64.

Bethmann, E. W.: *Bridge to Islam, a Study of the Religious Forces of Islam and Christianity in the Near East,* Nashville, Tenn., 1950.

Canaan, T.: *Mohammedan Saints and Sanctuaries in Palestine,* London 1927.

Canard, M.: "La Guerre sainte dans le monde islamique et le monde chrétien," in *2e Congrès de la Fédération des Sociétés Savantes de l'Afrique du Nord,* Alger 1936, 605–24.

Cragg, K.: *The Call of the Minaret,* N.Y. 1956.

Faris, N. A. (ed. and trans.) : *Arab Archery, An Arabic MS. of about 1500, "A Book of Excellence of the Bow and Arrow" and the Description thereof,* Princeton, N.J., 1945.

Gardet, L. and M. M. Anawati: *Introduction à la théologie musulmane, Essai de théologie comparée,* Paris 1948.

Gaudefroy-Demombynes, M.: *Les Institutions musulmanes,* rev. ed. Paris 1931; English trans. by J. R. McGregor: *Muslim Institutions,* London 1950.

————: *Le Pèlerinage à la Mekke,* Paris 1923.

Gibb, H. A. R.: *Whither Islam?* (Lecture by Massignon) , London 1952.

Goldziher, I.: *Vorlesungen über den Islam,* Heidelberg 1910; French trans. by J. Arin: *Le Dogme et la loi de l'Islam,* Paris 1920.

Grünebaum, G. E. von: *Medieval Islam,* Chicago 1946.

Lammens, H.: *L'Islam, croyances et institutions,* Beirut 1926; English trans. by E. Denison Ross: *Islam, Beliefs and Institutions,* London 1929.

LaMonte, J. L.: "Crusade and Jihad," in *The Arab Heritage,* ed. by N. A. Faris, Princeton, N.J., 1944, 159–98.

Levy, R.: *An Introduction to the Sociology of Islam*, 2 vols., London 1929.

Ritter, H.: "Kleine Mitteilungen und Anzeigen, 'La Parure d'Or des Cavaliers' und die Literatur über die ritterlichen Kunste," *Der Islam*, XVIII–1929, 116–54.

Schacht, J.: *The Origins of Muhammadan Jurisprudence*, Oxford 1950.

Tritton, A. S.: *The Caliphs and Their Non-Muslim Subjects*, Oxford 1930.

——: "Islam and the Protected Religions," *Journal of the Royal Asiatic Society*, 1931, 311–38.

Wensinck, A. J.: *The Muslim Creed, Its Genesis and Historical Development*, Cambridge 1932.

EGYPT AND SYRIA

Becker, Carl H.: *Beiträge zur Geschichte Aegyptens unter dem Islam*, 2 vols., Strasbourg 1902–03. (Fatimid history.)

Gaudefroy-Demombynes, M.: *La Syrie à l'époque des Mamelouks d'après les auteurs arabes, description géographique, économique et administrative*, Paris 1923.

Harris, G. L. (ed.): *Egypt* (Human Relations Area Files, Country Survey Series), New Haven, Conn., 1957.

Lane-Poole, S.: *History of Egypt in the Middle Ages*, new ed., London 1952.

——: *Saladin and the Fall of the Kingdom of Jerusalem*, new ed., London 1926.

Muir, W.: *The Mameluke or Slave Dynasty of Egypt (1260–1517)*, London 1896.

Popper, W.: *Egypt and Syria under the Circassian Sultans (1382–1468)*, *Systematic Notes to ibn Taghri Bardi's Chronicles of Egypt*, Berkeley, Calif., 1955.

——: *History of Egypt (1382–1411)*, trans. from Abul-Maḥāsin's *Annals*, 2 vols., Berkeley, Calif., 1954.

Quatremère, F.: *Histoire des sultans mamelouks*, 2 vols., Paris 1837–45. (This is part of Maqrizi's chronicle entitled "Kitāb al-Sulūk," ed. in progress by M. M. Ziada, Cairo 1934 ff.)

Stripling, G. W. F.: *The Ottoman Turks and the Arabs*, Urbana, Ill., 1942.

Weil, G.: *Geschichte des abbasidenchalifats in Egypten*, 2 vols., Stuttgart 1860–62.

Wiet, G.: *L'Égypte arabe, dès la conquête arabe à la conquête ottomane, 642–1517 de l'ère chrétienne* (*Histoire de la Nation Égyptienne,* IV) , Paris 1937.

————: *L'Egypte Musulmane dès la conquête arabe à la conquête ottomane* (*Précis de l'Histoire d'Égypte,* T. II, pt. 2) , Cairo 1932.

Zettersteen, K. V.: *Beiträge zur Geschichte der Mamlukensultane,* Leiden 1919.

Ziada, M. M: "The Mamluk Conquest of Cyprus in the XVth Century," *Bulletin of the Faculty of Arts* (Cairo University) , I–1933, 90–113.

THE TURKISH COUNTER-CRUSADE

Babinger, F. C.: *Beiträge zur Frühgeschichte des Turkenherrschaft in Rumelien (14.–15. Jahrhundert)* , Brünn 1944.

Gibbons, H. A.: *The Foundation of the Ottoman Empire: A History of the Osmanlis up to the Death of Bayezid I (1300–1403)* , Oxford 1916. (Excellent bibliography.)

Hammer-Purgstall, J. von: *Geschichte des osmanischen Reiches,* 10 vols., Pesth 1827–35; French ed. and trans. by J. J. Hellert: *Histoire de l'empire ottoman,* 18 vols., Paris 1835–43. (Wealth of Turkish authorities.)

Hasluck, F. W.: *Christianity and Islam under the Sultans,* ed. by Margaret M. Hasluck, 2 vols., Oxford 1929.

Jonquière, vicomte de la: *Histoire de l'empire ottoman,* new ed., 2 vols., Paris 1914.

Jorga, N.: *Geschichte des osmanischen Reiches nach den Quellen dargestellt,* 5 vols., Gotha 1908–13.

Kantemir, D.: *The History of the Growth of the Ottoman Empire,* trans. by N. Tindal, London 1735.

Knolles, R.: *The Generall Historie of the Turks,* London 1638.

Lybyer, A. H.: *The Government of the Ottoman Empire in the Time of Suleiman the Magnificent,* Cambridge, Mass., 1913.

Marriott, J. A. R.: *The Eastern Question,* 4th ed., Oxford 1940.

Merriman, Roger B.: *Suleiman the Magnificent 1520–66,* Cambridge, Mass., 1944. (Good notes and bibliography.)

Ohsson, M. d': *Tableau général de l'empire ottoman,* 7 vols., Paris 1788–1824; larger ed. of early portions in 3 vols., Paris 1787–1822.

Wittek, Paul: *Das Fürstentum Mentesche: Studien zur Geschichte*

Westkleinasiens im 13.–15. Jh., Istanbul 1934. (Turkish history in the 13th–15th centuries.)

Wittek, Paul: *The Rise of the Ottoman Empire,* London 1938.

Zinkeisen, J. W.: *Geschichte des osmanischen Reiches in Europa,* 7 vols., Hamburg and Gotha 1840–63. (Useful supplement to Hammer-Purgstall, particularly on diplomacy and the Mediterranean campaigns; employs Venetian sources.)

CONSTANTINOPLE

Baker, B. G.: *The Walls of Constantinople,* London 1910.

Barth, H.: *Constantinople* (Les Villes d'Art Célèbres), Paris 1906.

Besant, W.: *Constantinople—A Sketch of its History from its Foundation to its Conquest by the Turks in 1453,* London 1879.

Bréhier, L.: *Vie et mort de Byzance,* Paris 1947.

Bury, J. B.: "The Fall of Constantinople," *Yale Review,* N.S., III–1913–14, 56–77.

Clement, C. E.: *Constantinople, The City of the Sultans,* Boston 1895.

Dwight, H. G.: *Constantinople Old and New,* N.Y. 1915.

Ebersolt, J.: *Constantinople byzantine et les voyageurs du Levant,* Paris 1919.

Grosvenor, E. A.: *Constantinople,* 2 vols., Boston 1895.

Gurlitt, C.: *Konstantinopel,* Berlin 1908.

Hutton, W. H.: *Constantinople, The Story of the Old Capital of the Empire* (Medieval Towns Series), 3rd ed., London 1907.

Marriott, J. A. R.: *The Eastern Question,* 4th ed., Oxford 1940.

Milligen, A. van: *Byzantine Constantinople—The Walls of the City and Adjoining Historical Sites,* London 1899.

Oberhummer, E.: *Constantinoplis—Abriss der Topographie und Geschichte,* Stuttgart 1899.

Ostrogorsky, G.: *Geschichte des byzantinischen Staates,* Munich 1940; English trans. by Joan Hussey: *History of the Byzantine State,* Oxford 1956.

Pears, E.: *The Destruction of the Greek Empire and the Story of the Capture of Constantinople by the Turks,* London and N.Y. 1903.

Schlumberger, G.: *Le Siège, la prise et le sac de Constantinople par les Turcs en 1453,* Paris 1915.

Schultze, V.: *Konstantinopel,* Berlin 1913.

Vasiliev, A.: *History of the Byzantine Empire,* in 1 vol., Madison, Wisc., 1952.

Vast, H.: "Le Siège et la prise de Constantinople par les turcs," *R.H.,* XIII–1880, 1–40.

4. Romance Literature

Bastin, J., and E. Faral (eds.) : *Onze poèmes de Ruteboeuf concernant la croisade,* Paris 1946.

Bédier, J.: *Les Chansons de Croisade,* Paris 1909.

Boissanade, H.: *Du nouveau sur la Chanson de Roland,* Paris 1923.

Colleville, M.: *Les Chansons allemandes de croisade en moyen allemand,* Paris 1936. (After the Third Crusade.)

Duparc-Quioc, S.: "La Chanson de Jérusalem, Étude historique et critique," *E. de C.,* 1937, 137–43.

Hatem, A.: *Les Poèmes épiques des croisades,* Paris 1932.

Henne am Rhyn, O.: *Die Kreuzzüge und die Kultur ihrer Zeit,* Leipzig 1886.

————: *Kulturgeschichte des Kreuzzüge,* Leipzig 1894.

Kremer, A. von: *Kulturgeschichtliche Beziehungen zwischen Europa und dem Oriente,* Vienna 1876. (Short lecture.)

Paris, P. (ed.) : *La Chanson d'Antioche,* 2 vols., Paris 1848.

Roy, E.: "Les Poèmes français relatifs à la Ire. Croisade—Le poème de 1356 et ses sources," *Romania,* LV–1929, 411–68.

5. Military Orders of Religion

GENERAL WORKS

Belloy, P. de: *De l'origine et institution de divers ordres de chevalerie,* Paris 1613.

Favyn, A.: *Le Théatre de l'honneur de chevalerie,* 2 vols., Paris 1620.

Giustiniani, B.: *Historia cronologica dell' origine degli ordini militari e di tutte le religione cavalleresche,* 2 vols., Venice 1692.

Hélyot, P.: *Histoire des ordres monastiques, religieux et militaires, et de congrégations séculaires,* 8 vols., Paris 1711–21.

Hermant, G.: *Histoire des religions ou ordres militaires de l'église,* Rouen 1689.

Keightley, Th.: *Secret Societies of the Middle Ages,* London 1837. (Concerns Assassins, Templars, and secret tribunals of Westphalia.)

Mendo, A.: *De ordinibus militaribus disquisitio canonica,* Lyons 1668.

Migne, J. P.: *Dictionnaires des ordres religieux et militaires,* 4 vols., Paris 1859. (Based on Hélyot (see above) ; alphabetically arranged.)

Prutz, H.: *Der Anteil der geistlichen Ritterorden an dem geistigen Leben ihrer Zeit,* Munich 1908.

————: *Die geistlichen Ritterorden—ihre Stellung zur kirchlichen, politischen, gesellschaftlichen und wirtschaftlichen Entwicklung des Mittelalters,* Berlin 1908.

Woodhouse, F. C.: *The Military Religious Orders,* London 1879.

THE TEMPLARS

Albon, marquis d': *Cartulaire de l'Ordre du Temple* (to the year 1150), Paris 1913–22.

Campbell, G. A.: *The Knights Templars, Their Rise and Fall,* London 1937.

Carrière, V.: *Histoire et cartulaire des Templiers de Provins avec une introduction sur les débuts de Temple en France,* Paris 1919.

Curzon, H. du (ed.) : *La Règle du Temple,* Paris 1886.

Delisle, L.: "Opérations financières des Templiers," *Mon. et Mém.,* XXXIII–1889.

Dessubré, M.: *Bibliographie de l'ordre des Templiers,* Paris 1928.

Finke, H.: *Papsttum und Untergang des Templerordens,* 2 vols., Münster 1907.

Gmelin, J.: *Schuld oder Unschuld des Templerordens—Kritischer Versuch zur Lösung der Frange,* Stuttgart 1893.

Lambert, E.: *L'Architecture des Templiers,* Paris 1954.

Lavocat, L. L. L.: *Procès des frères de l'ordre du Temple,* Paris 1888.

Lea, H. C.: *History of the Inquisition,* 4 vols., N.Y. and London 1906–07; see Vol. III, ch. 5.

Lizerand, G.: "Les Dépositions du Grand Maître Jacques de Molay au procès des Templiers, 1307–14," *Le Moyen Âge,* XXVI–1913, 81–106.

—————— (ed.) : *Le Dossier de l'affaire des Templiers (Classiques de l'histoire de France au moyen âge,* II) , Paris 1923.

Lundgreen, F.: *Wilhelm von Tyrus und der Templerorden* (Dissert.) , Berlin 1911.

Martin, E. J.: *The Trial of the Templars,* London 1928.

Melville, M.: *La Vie des Templiers,* Paris 1951.

Prutz, H.: *Entwicklung und Untergang des Templerherrenordens,* Berlin 1888.

Rastoul, A.: *Les Templiers, 1118–1312,* 2nd ed., Paris 1905.

Schnürer, G.: *Die Ursprungliche Templerregel,* Fribourg i.B. 1903.

Schottmüller, K.: *Der Untergang des Templer-Ordens,* 2 vols., Berlin 1887.

Schüpferling, M.: *Der Templerherren Orden in Deutschland,* Bamberg 1915.

THE HOSPITALLERS—RHODES AND MALTA

Bedford, W. K. R., and R. Holbeche: *The Order of the Hospital of St. John of Jerusalem,* London 1902.

Bosio, I.: *Dell' istoria . . . religione . . . e milizia di S. Giovanni Gierosolimitano,* 3 vols., Rome 1594–1602; other editions— Rome 1621; Rome and Naples, 1629–34; Vol. III, Rome 1676, and Naples 1695.

Cohn, R.: *Knights of Malta 1523–1798,* London 1920.

Delaville LeRoulx, J.: *Cartulaire général des Hospitaliers de l'Ordre de Saint-Jean de Jérusalem (1100–1310),* 2 vols., Paris 1879–97.

—————— : *Les Hospitaliers à Rhodes jusqu'à la Mort de Philibert de Nailhac, 1310–1421,* Paris 1913.

—————— : *Les Hospitaliers en Terre Sainte et à Chypre, 1100–1310,* Paris 1904.

—————— : *Mélanges sur l'Ordre de S. Jean de Jérusalem,* Paris 1910.

Gabriel, Albert: *La Cité de Rhodes, MCCCX–MDXXII,* Paris 1921.

Ganem, Halil: *Les Sultans ottomans,* 2 vols., Paris 1901–02. (Information about the siege of Malta.)

King, E. J.: *The Knights Hospitallers in the Holy Land,* London 1931.

Kingsley, R. G.: *The Order of St. John of Jerusalem, Past and Present,* London 1919.

Parodi, E.: *Storia dei Cavalieri di S. Giovanni di Gerusalemme,* Bari 1907.

Porter, W.: *Knights of Malta or the Order of St. John of Jerusalem,* 2 vols., London 1858; 2nd ed. in 1 vol., 1884.

Seddall, Henry: *Malta,* London 1870. (About the siege of Malta.)

Symons-Jeune, J. F.: *Eight Hundred Years of the Order of the Hospital of St. John of Jerusalem,* London 1922.

Vertot, abbé: *Histoire des chevaliers de Malta,* 7 vols., Paris 1819.

6. The Art of War

Atiya, A. S.: *The Crusade in the Later Middle Ages,* London 1938.

Ayalon, D.: *Gunpowder and Firearms in the Mamluk Kingdom: A Challenge to a Medieval Society,* London 1956.

Boutaric, E.: *Institutions militaires de la France avant les armées permanentes,* Paris 1863.

Cahen, C.: "Un Traité d'armurérie composé pour Saladin," *Bulletin d'Études Orientales,* XII–1947–48, 103–63.

Creswell, K. A. C.: *Bibliography of Arms and Armour in Islam,* London 1956.

Delbruck, H.: *Geschichte des Kriegskunst im Rahmen der politischen Geschichte,* 7 vols., Berlin 1900–36.

Delpech, H.: *Tactique au Xe siècle,* 2 vols., Paris 1886.

Deschamps, P.: *Les Châteaux des croisés en Terre Sainte;* Vol. I: "Le Crac des chevaliers," Paris 1934; Vol. II: "La Défense du royaume de Jérusalem," Paris 1939.

Fedden, R.: *Crusader Castles: A Brief Study in the Military Architecture of the Crusaders,* London 1950. (Problems of castle building.)

Heermann, O.: *Die Gefechtsführung abendländischer Heere im Orient in der Epoche des ersten Kreuzzugs,* Marburg 1888.

Hime, H. W.: *The Origin of Artillery,* London 1915.

Jahn, H.: *Die Heereszahlen in der Kreuzzugen* (Dissert.), Berlin 1907.

Khaddūri, M.: *The Law of War and Peace in Islam,* London 1941.

Kohler, G.: *Die Entwickelung des Kriegswesens und der Kriegs-*

führung in der Ritterzeit von mitte des II. Jahrhunderts bis zu den Hussitenkriegen, 3 vols., Breslau 1886–90.

Lacabane, L.: "De la poudre à canon et son introduction en France," *E. de C.,* 2e sér., I–1844, 28–57.

Laking, G. F.: *A Record of European Armour and Arms through Seven Centuries,* 5 vols., London 1920–22.

Lawrence, T. E.: *Crusader Castles,* 2 vols., London 1936.

Lot, F.: *L'Art militaire et les armées au moyen âge,* 2 vols., Paris 1946.

Ludwig, F.: *Reise und Marschgeschwindigkeit in 12ten und 13ten Jahrhundert,* Berlin 1897.

Oman, C.: *The Art of War in the Sixteenth Century,* N.Y. 1937.

————: *History of the Art of War in the Middle Ages,* 2 vols., London 1924; rev. abridged ed. in 1 vol. by J. H. Beeler, N.Y. 1953.

Partington, J. R.: *A History of Greek Fire and Gunpowder,* Cambridge 1960.

Rey, E. G.: *Les Colonies franques de Syrie,* Paris 1883.

————: *Étude sur les monuments de l'architecture militaire des croisés en Syrie et dans l'île de Chypre,* Paris 1871.

Ritter, H.: "Kleine Mitteilungen und Anzeigen—'La Parure des Cavaliers' und die Literatur über die ritterlichen Kunste," *Der Islam,* XVIII–1929, 116–54.

Scanlon, George T. (ed. and trans.): 'Umar ibn Ibrahīm al-Awsi al-Anṣāri, *A Muslim Manual of War, being Tafrij al-Kurub fi Tadbir al-Hurub,* American University, Cairo 1961.

Smail, R. C.: "Crusaders' Castles in the Twelfth Century," *Cambridge Historical Journal,* X–1951, 133–49.

————: *Crusading Warfare (1097–1193),* Cambridge 1956.

7. Islamic Culture

This section stresses Arabic influence upon Western culture and draws on materials covering a wide expanse of time—pre-Islamic to late medieval—in line with the author's conception of the Crusade movement and the impact of Islam (see Preface).

GENERAL LITERATURE

Arberry, Arthur J.: *The Legacy of Persia,* Oxford 1953. (A series of essays on Persian culture and its influence on Persia's neighbors in pre-Islamic and Islamic times.)

Archer, J. C.: "Our Debt to Moslem Arabs," *The Moslem World*, XXIX–1939, 248–64.

Arnold, T., and A. Guillaume: *The Legacy of Islam*, Oxford 1931. (Invaluable on most aspects of Islamic culture.)

Atiya, A. S.: *Crusade, Commerce and Culture*, Bloomington, Ind., 1962. (See ch. 6.)

Chand, Tara: *Influence of Islam on Indian Culture*, Allahabad 1936. (Concentrates on religion and art; valuable bibliography.)

Daniel, N.: *Islam and the West—The Making of an Image*, Edinburgh 1960.

Dierks, F.: *Die Araber im Mittelalter und ihr Einfluss auf die Kultur Europas*, 2nd ed., Leipzig 1882.

———: *Die arabische Kultur in mittelalterlichen Spaniens*, Hamburg 1887.

Ganshof, F. L.: *Le Moyen Âge*, Paris 1953.

Gardet, L.: *La Cité musulmane, Vie sociale et politique*, Paris 1954.

Glanville, S. R. K. (ed.) : *The Legacy of Egypt*, Oxford 1942.

Grünebaum, Gustave E. von: *Islam: Essays in the Nature and Growth of a Cultural Tradition*, Menasha, Wisc., 1955.

———: *Medieval Islam, A Study in Cultural Orientation*, 2nd ed., Chicago 1953. (Predominantly literary and religious.)

———: *Unity and Variety in Muslim Civilization*, Chicago 1955. (An evaluation of the important relations between the universal Muslim culture pattern and the diverse local traditions of Islamic countries.)

Hell, J.: *Die Kultur der Araber*, new ed., Leipzig 1919; English trans. by S. Khuda Bukhsh, 2nd ed., Lahore 1943.

Hodgson, M. G. S.: *Introduction to Islamic Civilization, Course Syllabus and Selected Readings*, 3 vols., Chicago 1958–59.

Kremer, A. von: *Culturgeschichte des Orients unter den Chalifen*, 2 vols., Vienna 1875–77; English trans. in part by S. Khuda Bukhsh: *The Orient under the Caliphs*, Calcutta 1920.

———: *Culturgeschichtliche Streifzüge auf dem Gebiete des Islams*, Leipzig 1873; English trans. by S. Khuda Bukhsh: *Contributions to the History of Islamic Civilization*, Calcutta 1905.

Landau, R.: *Arab Contribution to Civilization*, San Francisco 1958.

———: *Islam and the Arabs*, N.Y. 1959.

Lane, E. W.: *Arabian Society in the Middle Ages,* ed. by S. Lane-Poole from his notes to the *Arabian Nights,* London 1883.

Le Bon, G.: *La Civilisation des arabes,* Paris 1884.

Lévi-Provençal, Évariste: *La Civilisation arabe en Espagne: vue générale,* Cairo 1938. (Short essay on Arab civilization in Spain and its contacts with and influence on Western civilization.)

————: *Islam d'Occident: études d'histoire médiévale,* Paris 1948. (Annotated edition of selected lectures and papers on various historical and cultural aspects of Islam in Spain and North Africa.)

Mazahéri, Aly: *La Vie quotidienne des musulmans au moyen âge,* 2 vols. (I, 8e au 9e siècle; II, 10e au 13e siècle), Paris 1951.

Mez, A.: *Die Renaissance des Islams,* Heidelberg 1922; English trans. by S. Khuda Bukhsh and D. S. Margoliouth, London 1938.

Risler, J. C.: *La Civilisation arabe,* Paris 1955.

Rosenthal, E.: "Traces of Arab Influence in Spain," *I.C.,* XI–1937, 324–40.

Sachau, E. C. (English trans.) : *Alberuni's India—An Account of the Religion, Philosophy, Literature, Geography, Chronology, Astronomy, Customs, Laws, and Astrology of India about 1030 A.D., with Notes and Indices,* 2 vols., London 1910.

Shushtery, A. M. A.: *Outlines of Islamic Culture,* 2 vols., Bangalore 1938.

Suter, H.: *Die Araber als Vermittler der Wissenschaften in ihrem Übergang vom Orient in den Occident,* 2nd ed., Aarau 1897.

Young, T. C.: "Christendom's Cultural Debt to Islam," *The Moslem World,* XXXV–1945, 89–110.

———— (ed.) : *Near Eastern Culture and Society, A Symposium of the Meeting of East and West,* Princeton, N.J., 1951.

PHILOSOPHY AND THEOLOGY

Anawati, G. C.: *Millénaire d'Avicenne, Essai de bibliographie avicennienne,* Cairo 1950.

Arberry, A. J.: *Revelation and Reason in Islam,* London 1957.

Asín Palacios, Miguel: *Algazel, dogmatica, moral, ascetica,* Saragossa 1901.

————: "El Averroísmo teológico de Santo Tomás de Aquino," *Homenaje a Codera,* 1904, 271–331. (Also see below, Literature.)

Avicenna Commemoration Volume (Iran Society) , Calcutta 1956.

Becker, C. H.: *Christentum und Islam,* Tübingen 1907; English trans. by H. J. Chaytor: *Christianity and Islam,* N.Y. 1909.

———: *Vom Werden und Wesen der islamischen Welt,* Leipzig 1924.

Bell, R.: *The Origin of Islam in Its Christian Environment,* London 1926.

———: *Introduction to the Qur'ān,* Edinburgh 1953.

Boer, T. de: *Geschichte der Philosophie im Islam,* Stuttgart 1901; English trans. by E. Jones: *The History of Philosophy in Islam,* London 1903.

Calverley, E. E.: *Al-Ghazzāli, Worship in Islam, being a Translation with commentary and introduction of al-Ghazzāli's Book of the Ihyā on the Worship,* Allahabad 1925.

Carra de Vaux, B.: *Algazali,* Paris 1902.

———: *Avicenne,* Paris 1900.

———: *Penseurs de l'Islam,* 5 vols., Paris 1921–28.

Dieterici, F.: *Alfarābi's philosophische Abhandlungen,* Leiden 1890.

Farrūkh, O. A.: *The Arab Genius in Science and Philosophy* (American Council of Learned Societies) , trans. by J. B. Hardie, Washington, D.C., 1954.

Flügel, G.: *Al-Kindi genant "der Philosoph der Araber,"* Leipzig 1857.

Gardet, L., and M. M. Arawati: *Introduction à la théologie musulmane,* Paris 1948.

Gauthier, L.: *Ibn Rochd (Averroes),* Paris 1948.

———: *Traité décisif sur l'accord de la religion et de la philosophie,* Arabic text and French trans., Algiers 1948, Cf. G. F. Hourani: *Kitāb Faṣl al-Maqāl,* text ibn Rushd, Leiden 1959; English trans. in progress.

Georr (Ghurr) , Khalil: *Bibliographie d'al-Farabi* (Dissert.) , Paris 1946.

Goichon, A. M.: *Lexique de la langue philosophique d'ibn Sīnā (Avicenne),* Paris 1938; Supp.: *Vocabulaires comparés d'Aristote et d'ibn Sīnā,* 1938.

———: *La Philosophie d'Avicenne et son influence en Europe médiévale,* Paris 1944.

Goldziher, I.: *Muhammedanische Studien,* 2 vols., Halle 1889–90.

Guillaume, A.: *The Traditions of Islam, An Introduction to the Study of the Hadith Literature*, Oxford 1924.

Hammond, R.: *The Philosophy of Alfarabi and Its Inflence on Medieval Thought*, N.Y. 1947.

Hartmann, R.: *Die Religion des Islam*, Berlin 1944.

Horten, M. J.: *Die Philosophie des Islams*, Munich 1924.

Husik, I.: *A History of Jewish Medieval Philosophy*, N.Y. 1916.

Kismet, A. L.: *A Study in Tolerance as Practised by Mohammed and His Immediate Successors*, N.Y. 1927.

Klibanski, R.: *The Continuity of Platonic Tradition*, London 1939.

Krausz, L.: "Farabi's Plato," in *Ginzberg Jubilee Volume* (American Academy for Jewish Research), N.Y. 1945, 357–94.

Macdonald, D. B.: *The Development of Muslim Theology, Jurisprudence and Constitutional Theory*, N.Y. 1903.

Müller, M. J.: *Philosophie und Theologie von Averroes*, Munich 1875.

Munk, S.: *Maimonides, le guide des égarés: traité de théologie et de philosophie*, Arabic text and French trans., 3 vols., Paris 1856–66; English trans. by M. Friedlander: *Guide to the Perplexed, by Moses ben Maimon, called Maimonides*, 3 vols., London 1885, 2nd ed. in 1 vol., London 1928.

————: *Mélanges de philosophie juive et arabe*, 2nd ed., Paris 1927.

Quadri, G.: *La Philosophie arabe dans l'Europe médiévale des origines à Averroes*, trans. by R. Huret, Paris 1947.

Renan, E.: *Averroes et l'Averroisme*, Paris 1861.

Salman, D.: "The Medieval Latin Translations of Alfarabi's Works," *New Scholasticism*, XIII–1939, 245–61.

Théry, G.: *Tolède, grande ville de la Renaissance médiévale*, Oran 1944.

Walzer, R.: *Alfarabius, De Platonis Philosophia*, London 1943.

————: "Arabic Transmission of Greek Thought to Medieval Europe," *Bulletin of the John Rylands Library*, XXIX–1945, 160 ff.

Wensinck, A. J.: *La Pensée de Ghazali*, Paris 1940.

Wise, S.: *Ibn Gabirol's (Avicenbron) Improvement on Moral Qualities*, N.Y. 1902.

Wittmann, M.: *Die Stellung des heiligen Thomas von Aquin zur*

Avencebrol (ibn Gabirol) (*Beiträge zur Geschichte der Philosophie des Mittelalters*), Münster 1905.

Wolfson, A.: "The Double Faith Theory in Clement, Saadya, Averroes and St. Thomas, and its Origin in Aristotle and the Stoics," *Jewish Quarterly Review,* XXXIII–1942, 213–64.

———: "The Kalam Arguments for Creation in Saadya, Averroes, Maimonides and St. Thomas," in *Saadya Anniversary Volume* (American Society for Jewish Research), N.Y. 1943, 198–245.

SCIENCE AND MATHEMATICS

Asín Palacios, Miguel: "Avempace Botanico," *Andalus,* V–1940, 255–99.

Ball, W. N. R.: *A Short Account of the History of Mathematics,* 4th ed., London 1908.

Berthelot, M., and M. Houdas: *La Chimie arabe,* Paris 1893.

Cantor, M.: *Vorlesungen über Geschichte der Mathematik,* 3rd ed., 4 vols., Leipzig 1898–1908; see Vol. I, chs. 32–37.

Catta, B., and A. N. Singh: *History of Hindu Mathematics,* Lahore 1935.

Coedes, G.: "À propos de l'origine des chiffres arabes," *Bulletin of the School for Oriental Research,* VI–1931, 323–38.

Colin, G. S.: "L'Origine grecque des 'chiffres de Fes' et de nos 'chiffres arabes'," *J.A.,* CCII–1933, 193–215.

Darmstaedter, E.: *Die Alchemie des Geber,* Berlin 1922.

Duhem, P.: *Le Système du Monde,* 5 vols., Paris 1913–17. (Cosmological theories.)

Haskins, C. N.: "Arabic Science in Western Europe," *Isis,* VII–1925, 478–86.

———: *Studies in the History of Medieval Science,* Cambridge, Mass., 1934.

Huemer, A.: "Die Einführung des dt.-arab. Zahlensystems in Frankreich und Deutschland," *Zeitschrift für die Österreich, Gymnasien* 1904.

al-Jahiz: *Kitāb al-Ḥayawān* (Book of Beasts), ed. by ʿAbd al-Salām Muḥammad Hārūn, 7 vols., Cairo 1938–47.

Jayakar: *Al-Damiri's Ḥayat al-Ḥayawān, A Zoological Lexicon,* 2 vols., London and Bombay 1906–08.

Jordan, L.: "Materialen zur Geschichte der arabischen Zahlzeichen in Frankreich," *Archiv für Kulturgeschichte,* III–1905, 155–95.

Lippmann, O. von: *Entstehung und Ausbereitung der Alchemie*, Berlin 1919.

Luckey, P.: *Tabit ibn Qurra über den geometrischen Richtigkeitsnachweis der Auflösung der quadratischen Gleichungen*, Leipzig 1941.

Meyerhof, M.: "Études de pharmacologie arabe, tirées de manuscrits inédits," *Bulletin de l'Institut d'Égypte*, XXII–1940, 133–52 and 157–62, and XXIII–1941, 13–29 and 89–101.

————: "On the Transmission of Greek and Indian Science to the Arabs," *I.C.*, II–1937, 17–29.

O'Leary, De Lacy: *Arabic Thought and Its Place in History*, London 1954.

————: *How Greek Science Passed to the Arabs*, London 1954.

Renan, E.: *L'Islamisme et la science*, Paris 1893.

Ruska, J.: *Arabische Alchemisten*, 2 vols., Heidelberg 1924.

————: *Zur ältesten arabischen Algebra und Rechnenkunst*, Heidelberg 1917.

Sánchez Pérèz, J. A.: *Biografías de matemáticos árabes que florecieron en España*, Madrid 1921.

Sarton, George: *Introduction to the History of Science*, 3 vols. in 5, Baltimore, Md., 1927–48.

Seligmann, R. (ed.) : *Abū Manṣūr Muwaffak, Liber fundamentorum pharmacologiae*, Vindobonae 1830–33.

Stephenson, J.: *Zoological Section of Nuzhatu-l-Qulūb of al-Qazwīni*, London 1928.

Taqi-al-Dīn al-Hilāli: *Einleitung zu al-Beirūni's Steinbuch*, Leipzig 1941.

Thorndike, L.: *History of Magic and Experimental Science*, 6 vols., Cambridge, Mass., 1927–41.

Wiedemann, E.: "Die Alchemie bei den Arabern," *Journal für praktische Chemie*, LXXVI–1907, 85–87 and 102–23.

————: *Zu Chemie bei den Arabern (Physikalische-medizinischen Soc. in Erlangen*, XLIII) , Erlangen 1911.

Wüstenfeld, F.: *Geschichte der arabischen Ärzte und Naturforscher*, Göttingen 1840.

ASTRONOMY AND ASTROLOGY

al-Biruni: *Book of Instruction in the Elements of the Art of Astrology*, Arabic text and English trans. by R. Ramsay Wright, London 1934.

Creswell, K. A. C.: "A Bibliography of Islamic Astrolabes," *Bulletin of the Faculty of Arts* (Cairo University), IX–1947–no. 2, 1–16.

Hartner, W.: "The Principle and Use of the Astrolabe," *Survey of Persian Art*, III–1939, 2530–54.

Krause, M.: *Die Sphärik des Menelaos aus Alexandrien in der Verbesserung von Abu Naṣr Manṣūr ibn ʿAli ibn ʿIrāq*, Berlin 1936.

Sauvaget, J.: "Sur d'anciennes instructions nautiques arabes pour les mers de l'Inde," *J.A.*, CCXXXVI–1948, 11–52.

Schirmer, O.: *Studien zur Astronomie der Araber*, Erlangen 1926.

Sédillot, J. J.: *Mémoires sur les instruments astronomiques des arabes*, Paris 1841–45.

Wiedemann, E.: "Zur Geschichte des Kompasses bei den Arabern," *Verhandlungen der deutschen physikalischen Gesellschaft zu Berlin*, IX–1907, 764–73.

MEDICINE

Bergstrasser, G.: *Hunain ibn Ishaq über die Syrischen und Arabischen Galenübersetzungen*, Leipzig 1925.

Campbell, D.: *Arabian Medicine and Its Influence on the Middle Ages*, 2 vols., London 1926.

Grüner, O. C.: *A Treatise on the Canon of Medicine*, London 1930.

Hirschberg, J.: *Geschichte der Augenheilkunde bei den Arabern*, Leipzig 1905.

Leclerc, L.: *Histoire de la Médicine Arabe*, 2 vols., Paris 1876.

————: *Traité des Simples par ibn al-Baithar*, 3 vols., Paris 1877.

Meyerhof, M.: "An Arabic Compendium of Medico-philosophical Definitions," *Isis*, X–1926, 340–49.

————: *The Book of the Ten Treatises on the Eye, by Hunain ibn Ishāq*, Cairo 1928.

————: "New Light on Hunain ibn Isḥāq," *Isis*, VIII–1926, 685–724.

Neuberger, M.: *Geschichte der Medizin*, 2 vols., Stuttgart 1906–11; English trans. by E. Playfair: *History of Medicine*, 2 vols., Oxford 1910–25.

Sarnelli, T.: *La Medicina araba*, Rome 1943.

Schacht, J., and M. Meyerhof: "The Medico-Philosophical Controversy between ibn Buṭlān of Baghdad and ibn Riḍwān of Cairo—A Contribution to the History of Greek Learning among the Arabs," *Bulletin of the Faculty of Arts* (Cairo University), 1937–no. 13.

ARTS AND ARCHITECTURE

Arnold, Sir Thomas W., and Alfred Guillaume (eds.) : *The Legacy of Islam*, Oxford 1931. (Selected essays. See A. H. Christie: "Islamic Minor Arts and Their Influence upon European Work"; Sir Thomas Arnold: "Islamic Art and its Influence on Painting in Europe"; and M. S. Briggs: "Architecture.")

Bréhier, L.: "L'Art roman du Puy et les influences islamiques," *J.S.*, 1935, 5–19.

Blochet, E.: *Musulman Painting XIIth–XVIIth Century,* English trans. by C. M. Benyon and Sir E. Denison Ross, London 1929.

Calvert, A. F.: *The Alhambra, Being a Brief Record of the Arabian Conquest of the Peninsula with a Particular Account of the Mohammedan Architecture,* London 1907.

————: *Moorish Remains in Spain, Being a Brief Record of the Arabian Conquest of the Peninsula with a Particular Account of the Mohammedan Architecture and Decoration in Cordova, Seville and Toledo,* London 1906.

Creswell, K. A. C.: *Early Muslim Architecture,* 4 vols., Oxford 1932–59. (Monumental work.)

Denison Ross, E. (ed.) : *The Art of Egypt,* London 1930.

Dimand, M. S.: *A Handbook of Mohammedan Decorative Arts,* N.Y. 1930.

Franz-Pascha, J.: *Die Baukunst des Islams,* Darmstadt 1896.

Gayet, A.: *L'Art arabe,* Paris n.d.

Glück, H., and E. Diez: *Die Kunst des Islam,* Berlin 1925.

Hassan, Zaky Mohamed: *Les Tulunides: étude de l'Égypte musulmane à la fin du IX siècle, 868–905,* Paris 1933. (Special attention given to art and architecture.)

Huyghe, R. (ed.) : *L'Art et l'homme,* 2 vols., Paris 1957–58; see Vol. II: G. Wiet, "L'Islam et l'art musulman," 1958, 148 ff.

Mâle, E.: "Les Influences arabes dans l'art roman," *Revue des Deux-Mondes,* 1923 (Nov.) , 311–44.

Marçais, G.: *L'Art de l'Islam,* Paris 1946.

Migeon, G.: *Manuel d'art musulman,* 2 vols., Paris 1907.

Pope, A. U.: *A Survey of Persian Art,* 6 vols., N.Y. 1938–39. (Monumental work.)

Whishaw, E. M.: *Arabic Spain, Sidelights on her History and Art,* London 1912.

PHILOLOGY

The larger dictionaries are indispensable. *E.g.,* E. W. Lane: *Arabic-English Lexicon,* reprinted N.Y. 1955; R. Dozy: *Supplément aux Dictionnaires Arabes,* Paris 1881; and A. Fischer, in progress under the auspices of the Arab Academy in Cairo.

Devic, L. M.: *Dictionnaire étymologique des môts français d'origine orientale,* Paris 1876.

Dozy, R., and W. Englemann: *Glossaire des môts espagnols et portugais dérivés de l'arabe,* 2nd ed., Leiden 1869.

Eguilaz, D. L. de: *Glosario etymologico de las palabras españolas de origen oriental,* Granada 1886.

Kopf, L.: "The Treatment of Foreign Words in Mediaeval Arabic Lexicology," in *Scripta Hierosolymitana,* ed. by Uriel Heyd (*Studies in Islamic History and Civilization,* published under the auspices of the Hebrew University, School of Oriental Studies, IX) Jerusalem 1961, 191–205.

Kunitzsch, P.: *Arabische Sternnamen in Europa,* Wiesbaden 1959.

Lammens, H.: *Remarques sur les môts français dérivés de l'arabe,* Beirut 1890.

Littmann, E.: *Morgenländische Wörter im Deutschen,* Tübingen 1924.

Lokotsch, L.: *Etymologisches Wörterbuch der europaischen Wörter orientalischen Ursprungs,* Heidelberg 1927.

Pérès, H.: "La Langue arabe et les habitants de l'Andalousie au moyen âge," *Revue de l'Académie Arabe,* XIX–1944, 393–408.

Steiger, A.: "Contribución a la fonética del Hispano-Arabe y de los Arabismos en el Ibero-Románico y el Siciliano," *Revista de Filología Española—Anejo,* XVII–1932.

LITERATURE

Abd-el-Jalil, J. M.: *Histoire de la littérature arabe,* Paris 1960.

Asín Palacios, M.: *El mistico murciano Abenarabi,* 4 vols., Madrid 1925–28.

————: *La Escatología musulmana en la Divina Commedia*, Madrid 1919; abridged English trans. by H. Sunderland: *Islam and the Divine Comedy*, London 1926.

Browne, E. G.: *A Literary History of Persia*, 4 vols., Cambridge 1928.

Ecker, L.: *Arabischer, provenzalischer und deutscher Minnegesang, ein motivgeschichtliche Untersuchung*, Bern 1934.

Erekmann, R.: "Der Einfluss der arabischspanischen Kultur auf die Entwickelung der Minnegesangs," *Deutsche Vierteljahrschrift*, IX–1931, 240–84.

Gabriele, F.: *La Poesía araba e la poesia occidentale*, Rome 1943; new ed. (*Storia e cività musulmana*), Rome 1947.

Gibb, E. J. W.: *A History of Ottoman Poetry*, 6 vols., London 1900–09.

Gibb, H. A. R.: *Arabic Literature, An Introduction*, Oxford 1926.

Gonzáles Palencía, A.: *Historia de la Literatura arabico-española*, Barcelona 1928.

Grünebaum, G. E. von: "The Arab Contribution to Troubadour Poetry," *Bulletin of the Iranian Institute*, VI–1946, 117–28.

Ḥusain ʿAli-Khān: "ʿUmar Khayyām and Some of his English Translators," *I.C.*, XXII–1948, 18–41.

Las Cajigas, I. de: *Los Mozarabes*, 2 vols., Madrid 1948.

————: *Los Mudejares*, Madrid 1948.

Levi della Vita, G.: "Nuova luce sulle fonti islamiche della Divina Commedia," *Andalus*, XIV–1949, 377–408.

Menéndez Pidal, R.: "Poesía árabe y poesía europea," *Bulletin Hispanique*, XL–1939, 337–423.

Nicholson, R. A.: *Eastern Poetry and Prose*, Cambridge 1922.

————: *A Literary History of the Arabs*, 2nd ed., London 1930.

————: *Studies in Islamic Mysticism*, Cambridge 1921.

————: *Studies in Islamic Poetry*, 2nd ed., London 1930.

Nykl, A. R.: *Hispano-Arabic Poetry and Its Relations with the Old Provençal Troubadours*, Baltimore, Md., 1946.

————: *Selections from Hispano-Arabic Poetry*, Beirut 1949.

Pérès, Henri: "La Poésie arabe d'andalousie et ses relations possibles avec la poésie des troubadours," *L'Islam et l'Occident, Cahiers du Sud*, Marseilles and Paris 1947.

Schack, A. F. von: *Poesie und Kunst der Araber in Spanien und Sizilien*, 2nd ed., 2 vols., Stuttgart 1877; Spanish trans. by J. Valera, 3 vols., Madrid 1893.

Singer, S.: *Arabische und europaische Poesie im Mittelalter,* Berlin 1918.

Spies, Otto: *Der Orient in der deutschen Literatur* (Berckers kleine Volksbibliothek), Kevelaer am Rh. 1949.

Steinschneider, M.: *Die arabische Literatur der Juden,* Frankfurt 1902.

EDUCATION

Flügel, G.: "Die grammatischen Schulen der Araber, nach den Quellen bearbeitet," *Abhandlungen für die Kunde des Morgenlandes,* II, pt. 4, Leipzig 1862.

Gudemann, M.: *Das judische Unterrichtswesen während der spanisch-arabischen Periode,* Vienna 1873.

Ḥamīdullah, M.: "Educational System in the Time of the Prophet," *I.C.,* XIII–1939, 48–59.

Haneberg, D.: *Abhandlungen über das Schul-und Lehrwesen der Muhamedaner im Mittelalter,* Munich 1850.

Heyworth-Dunne, J.: *An Introduction to the History of Modern Education in Egypt,* London 1939.

Khān, Muʿīd: "The Muslim Theories of Education during the Middle Ages," *I.C.,* XVIII–1944, 418–33.

Ribera, J.: *La Enseñanza entre los musulamanes españoles,* Saragossa 1896.

Talas, A.: *La Madrassa Nizamiya et son histoire,* Paris 1939.

Tawfīḳ, M. A.: "A Sketch of the Idea of Education in Islam," *I.C.,* XVII–1943, 317–26.

Tritton, A. S.: *Materials on Muslim Education in the Middle Ages,* London 1957.

Wüstenfeld, F.: *Die Akademien der Araber und ihre Lehrer,* Göttingen 1837.

8. East-West Commerce

TRADE

For the fullest classified bibliography on trade, with special reference to the Italian communes, see the works of Sapori, Heyd, and Lopez and Raymond (below). The following is a representative selection.

Aghnides, N.: *Mohammadan Theory of Finances,* N.Y. 1916.

Atiya, A. S.: *Crusade, Commerce and Culture,* Bloomington, Ind., 1962.

Babelon, E.: *Du commerce des arabes dans le nord de l'Europe avant les croisades,* Paris 1882.

Bratianu, G. I.: *Recherches sur le commerce génois dans la mer noire au XIIIe siècle,* Paris 1929.

Costello, L. S.: *Jacques Coeur,* London 1847.

Dopsch, A.: *Wirtschaftliche und soziale Grundlagen der europaischen Kulturentwicklung aus der Zeit von Caesar bis auf Karl den Grossen,* 2nd ed., 2 vols., Vienna 1923–24; abridged in 1 vol. by E. Patzelt, with English trans. by M. G. Beard and N. Marshall: *Economic and Social Foundations of European Civilization,* London 1937.

Evans, A. (ed.) : Francesco Balducci Pegolotti, *La Practica della Mercatura* (M.A.A.) , Cambridge, Mass., 1936. (Written in first half of 14th century.)

Fischel, W. J.: *Jews in the Economic and Political Life of Mediaeval Islam* (Royal Asiatic Society, monog. 22) , London 1937.

Foster, W.: *England's Quest of Eastern Trade,* London 1933.

Gaudefroy-Demombynes, M.: "Sur quelques ouvrages de hisba," *J.A.,* CCXXX–1938, 449–57.

Heyd, W.: *Geschichte des Levantehandels im Mittelalter,* 2 vols., Stuttgart 1879; standard French trans. by Furcy Reinaud and author: *Histoire du commerce du Levant au moyen âge,* 2 vols., Paris 1885–86; lithographed ed., Leipzig 1936, reprinted 1959.

Jacob, G.: *Der nordisch-baltische Handel der Araber im Mittelalter,* Leipzig 1887.

————: *Welche Handelsartikel bezogen die Araber des Mittelalters aus den nordisch-baltischen Landern?,* 2nd ed., Berlin 1891.

Kerr, A. B.: *Jacques Coeur,* London 1927.

Knight, M. M.: *Economic and Social History of Europe to the End of the Middle Ages,* Boston 1926.

Lane, F. C.: *Andrea Barbarigo, Merchant of Venice 1418–1449* (*The Johns Hopkins University Studies in Historical and Political Science,* LXII, no. 1,) Baltimore, Md., 1944.

Lewis, B.: "The Islamic Guilds," *E.H.R.,* VIII–1937, 20–37.

Lopez, R. S., and I. A. Raymond: *Medieval Trade in the Mediterranean—Illustrative Documents, trans. with Introduction and Notes (Records) ,* N.Y. 1955.

Lybyer, A. H.: "The Ottoman Turks and the Routes of Oriental Trade," *E.H.R.*, XXX–1915, 577–78.

Macpherson, D.: *Annals of Commerce*, 4 vols., London 1805. (Old but still useful.)

Mas Latrie, L. de: *Traités de paix et de commerce et documents divers contenant les relations des chrétiens avec les arabes d'Afrique septentrionale au moyen âge*, Paris 1866; Supp., 1872.

Mollat, M.: *Les Affaires de Jacques Coeur, Journal du procureur Dauvet*, 2 vols., Paris 1952–53.

Olwer, L. Nicolau d': *L'Expansio de Catalunya en la Mediterranea Oriental*, Barcelona 1926.

Pigeonneau, H.: *Histoire du commerce de la France*, 2 vols., Paris 1887–89.

Pirenne, H.: *Economic and Social History of Medieval Europe*, 5th ed., N.Y. 1937.

Postan, M., and E. E. Rich (eds.) : *Trade and Industry in the Middle Ages* (*The Cambridge Economic History of Europe*, II) , Cambridge 1952.

Prestage, E.: *The Portuguese Pioneers*, London 1933.

Ritter, H.: "Ein arabisches Handbuch der Handelswissenschaft," *Der Islam*, VII–1917, 1–91.

Sapori, A.: *Le Marchand italien au moyen âge*, Paris 1952.

Schaube, A.: *Handels-geschichte der romanischen Volker des Mittelmeergebiets bis zum Ende der Kreuzzüge*, Munich and Berlin 1906.

Thompson, J. W.: *An Economic and Social History of Europe in the Later Middle Ages (1300–1530)* , N.Y. 1931.

——: *Economic and Social History of the Middle Ages (300–1300)* , N.Y. 1928.

Wood, A. C.: *A History of the Levant Company*, London 1935.

Yver, G.: *Le Commerce et les Marchands dans l'Italie méridionale au XIIIe Siècle*, Paris 1903.

MEDITERRANEAN SHIPPING AND NAVAL HISTORY

Also see above, section III. 4.

Byrne, E. H.: *Genoese Shipping in the 12th and 13th Centuries* (M.A.A.) , Cambridge, Mass., 1930.

Caro, G.: *Genua und die Mächte am Mittelmeer (1257–1311)*, 2 vols., Halle 1895–99.

Chevalier, E.: *Histoire de la marine française depuis les débuts de la monarchie jusqu'au traité de paix de 1763*, Paris 1902.

Heyck, E.: *Genua und seine Marine im Zeitalter der Kreuzzüge*, Innsbruck 1886.

Jourdain, C.: "Mémoire sur les commencements de la marine militaire sous Philippe le Bel," *Mon. et Mém.*, XXX–1881, pt. 1, 377–418.

La Roncière, C.: *Histoire de la marine française*, 5 vols., Paris 1888–1920.

Lane, F. C.: *Venetian Ships and Shipbuilding of the Renaissance*, Baltimore, Md., 1934.

Manfroni, C.: *Storia della marina italiana (1261–1453)*, 2 vols., Leghorn 1902.

———: *Storia della Marina Italiana dalle invasione barbariche al trattato di Ninfeo (1261)*, Leghorn 1899.

Tramond, J.: *Manuel d'Histoire maritime de la France*, Paris 1916.

ARAB SHIPPING AND NAVAL HISTORY

Ehrenkreutz, A. S.: "The Place of Saladin in the Naval History of the Mediterranean Sea in the Middle Ages," *Journal of the American Oriental Society*, LXXV–1955, 100–16.

Fahmy, A. M.: *Muslim Sea Power in the Eastern Mediterranean, from the 7th to the 10th Century* A.D. (Dissert., published under auspices of Ministry of Education), Cairo 1950.

Hourani, G. F.: *Arab Seafaring in the Indian Ocean in Ancient and Early Medieval Times*, Princeton, N.J., 1951.

Kindermann, H.: "*Schiff*" *im Arabischen, Untersuchung über Vorkommen und Bedeutung der Termini*, Zwickau i. Sa. 1934.

Lewis, A. R.: *Naval Power and Trade in the Mediterranean (500–1100)*, Princeton, N.J., 1951.

Lewis, N.: *By Arab Dhow through the Red Sea*, London 1938.

TURKISH SHIPPING AND NAVAL HISTORY

Khalīfah, Ḥajji: *Tuḥfat al-Kibār* (History of the Maritime Wars of the Turks), English trans. by J. Mitchell, London 1831.

Re'is, Piri (d. 1554): *Bahrije—Das turkische Segelhandbuch für das mittelländische Meer vom Jahre 1521,* text and German trans., 2 vols., Berlin and Leipzig 1926–27.

9. Geography, Travel, and Atlases

Also see above, Monumental Collections, Additional Notes to section VII.

Abel, F. M.: *Géographie de la Palestine,* 2 vols., Paris 1933–38. *Atlas Vetus Terrae Sanctae, Ancient Maps of the Holy Land,* Jerusalem 1958.

Beazley, Sir C. R.: *The Dawn of Modern Geography,* 3 vols., London 1897–1906; later ed., N.Y. 1949.

Beckingham, C. F.: *Atlas of the Arab World and Middle East,* London 1960.

Biblioteca Geographorum Arabicorum, ed. by M. J. de Goeje, 6 vols., Leiden 1870–1927. (The basic starting point in the study of Arab geography and the contribution of Arab geographers. See above, Monumental Collections, section VII, for analysis and Additional Notes.)

Birot, P., and J. Dresch: *La Méditerranée et le Moyen-Orient,* 2 vols., Paris 1955; includes "Orbis—Introduction aux études de géographie.")

Blachère, R.: *Extraits des principaux géographes arabes du moyen âge,* Paris 1932.

Caroli a Santo Paulo: *Geographia sacra, cum notae animadversionibus lucae Holstenii,* Amsterdam 1704.

Carte dressée et publiée par le Bureau Topographique des Troupes Françaises du Levant, Beirut 1936.

Clermont-Ganneau, C.: *Archaeological Researches in Palestine during the years 1873–74,* 2 vols., London 1890–96.

Conder, C. R., and H. H. Kitchener: *Survey of Western Palestine —Memoirs of the Topography, Orography, Hydrography and Archaeology,* 3 vols., London 1881–83.

Droysens, G.: *Allgemeiner historische Handatlas,* Bielefeld and Leipzig 1886.

Dussaud, R.: *Topographie historique de la Syrie antique et médiévale,* Paris 1927.

———, P. Deschamps, and H. Seyrig: *La Syrie antique et médiévale illustrée,* Paris 1918.

Ebersolt, J.: *Constantinople byzantine et les voyageurs au Levant,* Paris 1918.

Enlart, D.: *Les Monuments des croisés dans le royaume de Jérusalem,* Paris 1926–27.

L'Extrême Orient au moyen âge, d'après les mss. d'un Flamand de Belgique, moine de Saint-Bertin à Saint-Omer et d'un prince d'Arménie, moine de Prémontre à Paris, ed. by L. de Backer, Paris 1877.

Grant, C. P.: *The Syrian Desert,* London 1937.

Guérin, M. V.: *Description géographique, historique et archéologique de la Palestine; Description de la Galilée,* 2 vols., Paris 1880.

Hazard, Harry W., and Hereward L. Cooke: *Atlas of Islamic History,* 3rd ed., Princeton, N.J., 1954. (Mainly concerned with the borders between Islam and Christendom. This and the work of Roolvink *et al.* are the only available general atlases of Islamic history.)

Hellert, J. J.: *Nouvel Atlas phisique, politique et historique de l'empire ottoman,* Paris 1844.

Issawi, C.: "Arab Geography and the Circumnavigation of Africa," *Osiris,* X–1952, 117 ff.

Jirecek, C. J.: *Die Heerstrasse von Belgrad nach Constantinopel und die Balkanpasse,* Prague 1877.

Jondet, G.: *Atlas historique de la ville et porte d'Alexandrie,* Cairo 1921.

Kahle, P.: *Die vorschollene Columbus-Karte vom 1498 in einer türkischen Weltkarte von 1513,* Berlin and Leipzig 1933.

Kamāl, Youssef: *Monumenta cartographica Africae et Aegypti,* 15 vols., Paris 1926–38. (Lavish publication containing full-size reproductions in color of maps from both Western and Oriental sources.)

Kammerer, A.: *La Mer Rouge, l'Abyssinie et l'Arabie depuis l'Antiquité,* Cairo 1929.

Lammens, H.: *Le Berceau d'Islam,* Rome 1914.

Lands of the Bible To-day, with Historical Notes and Map (compiled by National Geographic Society), Washington, D.C., 1956.

Lane-Poole, R.: *Historical Atlas of Modern Europe from the Decline of the Roman Empire,* Oxford 1902.

Le Strange, Guy: *Baghdad during the Abbasid Caliphate, from Contemporary Arabic and Persian Sources,* London 1924.

Le Strange, Guy: *The Geographical Part of "Nuzhat al-Qulūb"
composed by Hamd-Allah Mustawfi of Qazim in 740* A.H./*1340*
A.D., 2 vols., London 1915–19.

———: *The Lands of the Eastern Caliphate: Mesopotamia, Persia
and Central Asia, from the Moslem conquest to the time of
of Timur,* Cambridge 1930.

———: *Mukaddasi's Description of Syria and Palestine,* trans.
from Arabic, London 1892.

———: *Palestine under the Moslems,* Cambridge 1930. (Based on
careful study of Arabic and Persian sources.)

Marmarji, A. Sebastianus (ed. and trans.) : *Textes géographiques
arabes sur la Palestine,* Paris 1951. (Collection of translations
of Arabic texts.)

Maspéro, J., and G. Wiet: *Matériaux pour servir à la géographie
de l'Égypte,* Cairo 1914.

Matković, P.: *Reisen durch die Balkanhalbinsel während des
Mittelalters,* German trans. by J. S. Knapp (*Mitteilungen der
Geographischen Gesellschaft zu Wien,* XXIII) , Vienna 1880.
(Describes routes of First Crusade.)

Meer, F. van der: *Atlas of Western Civilization,* English version
by T. A. Birrell, Amsterdam 1954. (Contains introductions and
is profusely illustrated.)

Miller, K.: *Mappae Arabicae, Arabische Welt- und Länderkarten
der 9.–13. Jahrhunderts in Arabischer Überschaft, Lateinischer
Transkription und Übertragung, in Neuzeitliche Kartenskiz-
zen, mit Einleitenden Texten,* Stuttgart 1926 ff.

Minorsky, V. (ed. and English trans.) : *Shareef al-Zamān Tāhir
Marvazi on China* (c. 1120) , London 1942.

Nafis, Ahmad: *Muslim Contribution to Geography,* Lahore 1947.

*Oxford Regional Economic Atlas: The Middle East and North
Africa,* Oxford 1960.

Palestine of the Crusades, Map by C. N. Johns (Department of
Survey, Palestine Government) , Jerusalem 1938.

Palmer, R. A. (ed.) : *Rand McNally's Atlas of World History,*
N.Y. 1957.

Ramsay, W. M.: *The Historical Geography of Asia Minor,* London 1890.

*Recueil de voyages et de documents pour servir à l'histoire de la
géographie depuis le XIIIe jusqu'à la fin du XVI siècle,* publié

sous la direction de Ch. Schéfer et Henri Cordier, 22 vols., Paris 1882–1908; T. II: "Le Voyage de la sainct cyté de Hieru-salem avec la description des lieux, portz, villes, citez et aultres passaiges, fait l'an 1480, estant le siège du Grand Turc à Rhodes et regnant en France Loys unzième de ce nom," 1882; T. V: "Le Voyage et itinéraire d'outre-mer faict par frère Jehan Thenaud. Égypte, Syrie, Terre-Sainte," 1884; T. VIII: "Le Voyage de Monsieur d'Aramon, ambassadeur pour le Roy en Levant escript par noble homme Jean Chesneau, l'un des secré-taires dudict Seigneur ambassadeur," 1887; T. IX: "Les Voyages de Ludovico di Varthema, ou le Viateur, en la plus grande partie d'Orient. Traduits de l'italien en français par J. Balarin de Raconis," 1880; T. X: "Les Voyages en Asie au XIV siècle du bienheureux frère Odoric de Pordenone, religieux de Saint-François. Avec gravures et cartes," 1861; T. XI: "Le Voyage de la Terre-Sainte, composé par maistre Denis Possot, et achevé par messire Charles Philippe, seigneur de Champarmoy et de Grand-champ (1532)," 1890; T. XII: "Le Voyage d'outre-mer de Bertrandon de la Broquière, premier écuyer tranchant et con-seiller de Philippe, duc de Bourgogne," 1892; T. XIII–XV: "De-scription de l'Afrique, tièrce partie du monde, escrite par Jean-Leon-African, premièrement en langue arabesque, puis en toscane, et à present mise en français," 3 vols, 1897; T. XVI: "Voyage dans le Levant, par Dufresne Canaye (1573). Avec cartes et planches," 1899; T. XVII: "Itinéraire de Jerome Maurand. D'Antibes à Constantinople (1544). Texte italien. Avec 20 planches." 1901.

Röhricht, R.: *Bibliotheca Geographica Palaestina,* Berlin 1890. (Contains a full register of maps of the Holy Land from 333 A.D. to 1878, in a special section entitled "Cartographia," 598–662.)

Roolvink, R., Roelof, *et al.: Historical Atlas of the Muslim Peo-ples,* Amsterdam 1957. (Devotes much attention to internal de-velopments of the Muslim world.)

Sacy, S. de: *La Relation de l'Égypte de Abdellatif, savant de Bagdad (d.* 1231 A.D.), Paris 1810.

Salmon, F. J.: "A Map of Palestine of the Crusades," *Palestine Exploration Quarterly,* 1939 (July), 144–51.

Schwarz, Paul: *Iran im Mittelalter nach den arabischen Geogra-phen,* 9 vols., Leipzig and Stuttgart 1910–36. (Detailed description of Persia in the Middle Ages according to Arab geographers.)

Shepherd, W. R.: *Historical Atlas*, 8th rev. ed., N.Y. 1956.

Shucair, Naum: *History and Geography of the Sudan* (Arabic), 3 vols., Cairo 1903.

Smith, G. A.: *The Historical Geography of the Holy Land*, 26th ed., London 1935.

Speed, J.: *The Theatre of the Empire of Great Britain—together with a Prospect of the Most Famous Parts of the World, viz., Asia, Europe, America.* . . . , London 1676.

Sprüner, K. V., and Th. Mencke: *Hand-Atlas für die Geschichte des Mittelalters und der neuen Zeit*, Gotha 1880.

Survey of Palestine in 14 Sheets, Jerusalem 1935–37.

Tomaschek, W.: *Zur historischen Topographie von Kleinasien in Mittelalter* (*Sitzungsberichte der kaiserlichen Akademie der Wissenschaften*, CXXIV) , Vienna 1891.

Toussoun, Omar: *Historical Atlas of Lower Egypt from the first Hijra century/7th century* A.D. (Arabic) , Cairo 1934.

Villamont, Jacques de: *Les Voyages du Seigneur de Villamont* [en Italie, Grèce, Terre-Sainte, Égypte et autres lieux] . . . *divisez en trois livres* . . . *plus un abrégé de la description de toute la France*, reveu, corrigé, et augmenté de nouveau, Arras 1598; rev. ed., Paris 1600; new ed., Arras 1605; rev. ed., 1606; rev. ed., 1607; augmentez en ceste dernière Édition de son Secõd Voyage et du dessein de son Troisiesme, 2 pts., Paris 1609; rev. ed., Rouen 1618; troisième ed., Paris 1698.

Westerman's Atlas zur Weltgeschichte, new ed. by H. E. Stier et al., Berlin 1956.

Wright, J. K.: *The Geographical Lore of the Time of the Crusades*, N.Y. 1925.

Index

Académie des Inscriptions et des Belles-Lettres, 20 ff, 35

Africa. *See* geography

Antioch, First Crusade, 31 ff, 109–13; other source materials, 52 ff. *See also* assises

Arabs. *See* Crusade histories; Islam

architecture. *See* arts and architecture

Archives de l'Orient Latin, 52–57

Armenia, aftermath of Crusade, 53 ff. *See also* Christianity; Crusade histories

arts and architecture, Islamic influence, 155–56. *See also* pilgrimage

Asia, 44. *See also* geography; Mongols and missions

assises, de Jérusalem, 20, 33–34; de Romanie, 20, 34; d'Antioche, 21, 34

astrology. *See* astronomy and astrology

astronomy and astrology, Islamic influence, 153–54

Benedictines. *See* Saint-Maur

Berthereau, Dom Georges-François. *See* Saint-Maur

bibliography, general works, Western, 28, 79–80; Arabic and Oriental, 81–83

Bibliotheca Geographorum Arabicorum, 73–77

Bibliothèque des Croisades, 60–70. *See also* Michaud

Bongars. *See Gesta Dei per Francos*

Byzantium. *See* chronography and chronology; Church; Constantinople; Crusade histories (Greek)

Cathay. *See* geography; Mongols and missions

China. *See* geography; Mongols and missions

Christianity. *See* Church

chronicles, analyses by Michaud in *Bibliothèque des Croisades*, 60 ff; de France, 60–65; de France, d'Italie, et d'Angleterre, 65–67; d'Allemagne et du Nord de l'Europe, diverses, Grecques, Turques, et Arméniennes, 67–69; by Reinaud in *Bibliothèque des Croisades*, from Arabic mss., 69–70. *See also* Crusade; Crusade histories

chronography and chronology, 35; Western and Crusading, 84; Byzantine, 84–85; Arabic and Oriental, 85–86

chronology. *See* chronography and chronology

Church, Roman, 86–88, 115, 118, 122; Byzantine, 88–90; Near Eastern, 96–98

Cilicia. *See* Armenia

commerce, East-West, 158–60; illustrative documents, 71; Mediterranean shipping 90, 160–61; Arab shipping, 161; Turkish shipping, 161–62

Constantinople, relics, 57 ff; hagiography, 57–59; liturgy, 57, 59; siege of 1453, 64; Fourth Crusade, 57, 71, 118–22; aftermath of Crusade, 142–43. *See also* Crusade histories (Greek)

Copts, Coptic Christian Church, 96–98

Counter-Crusade, 138–40; Egyptian, 140–41; Turkish, 141–42

Crusade, general history of Latin Orient, 98 ff; background, 107–109; First Crusade, 109–13; Second Crusade, 113–15; Third Crusade, 115–17; Henry VI, 117–18; Fourth Crusade, 118–22; Children's Crusade, 122; Fifth Crusade, 122–24; Sixth Crusade, 124–25; Seventh and Eighth Crusades, 125–27; Later Crusade, 127–38; aftermath of Crusade (Counter-Crusade; Egypt and Syria; Turkey; Constantinople), 138–43

Crusade histories, Western (First Crusade), 29–32, 70–72; Oriental (and Arabic), 34–39, 69–70, 71, 116; Cypriot, 45, 55, 71; Greek, 40–41, 67–69; Armenian (and Syriac), 42–47, 67–69; Hebrew, 47; French, 60–65, 70–72; Italian, 65–67; English, 65–67, 70, 115–16; German (and Northern European), 67–69, 71, 116; Turkish, 67–69; Slavic, 71; Spanish, 71. *See also* Crusade

culture, Islamic, 147–58

Cyprus, aftermath of Crusade, 55 ff, 136–38. *See also* Crusade histories

Duchesne, André and François, *Historiae francorum* . . . , 61–63

education, Islamic influence, 158

Egypt and Syria, Arabic sources on Crusade, 35–39; aftermath of Crusade, 140–41

England. *See* Crusade histories

Europe, general histories, 86

Exuviae Sacrae Constantinopolitanae, 57–59

France. *See* Crusade histories

Genoa. *See* commerce (Mediterranean shipping)
geography, 73–77, 162–66; geographical dictionaries, 76; unpublished materials, 77. *See also* pilgrimage
Germany. *See* Crusade histories
Gesta Dei per Francos, 19; analysis, 60–61
Greece. *See* Byzantium

Hebrews. *See* Crusade histories
Henry VI. *See* Crusade
Histoire des Croisades. See Michaud
Histoire Littéraire de la France. See Saint-Maur
historians. *See* Crusade histories
historiography, Crusade, 17–28; Western bibliography, 24–26; Arabic and Oriental bibliography, 26–28
Holy Places. *See* pilgrimage
Hospitallers. *See* military orders

India. *See* geography
Islam, 91–96; and Crusade, 98–127; and Later Crusade, 127–38; Counter-Crusade, 138–43; art of war, 146–47; cultural influence on West, 147–58; East-West commerce, 158–62. *See also* Crusading histories; geography
Italy. *See* commerce (Mediterranean shipping) ; Crusade histories

Jerusalem, First Crusade 29 ff;

Jerusalem *(Continued)*
assises, 33–34; pilgrimage to, 47 ff. *See also* Latin Orient

LaMonte, John L. *See* Pennsylvania *History of the Crusades*
Latin Orient, 98–127. *See also* assises
laws. *See* assises
Lesser Armenia (La Petite Arménie) . *See* Armenia
literature, Romance, 143; Islamic influence, 156–58
Lusignans. *See* Armenia; Cyprus

Malta. *See* military orders (Hospitallers)
Mamluks. *See* Counter-Crusade (Egyptian) ; Islam
Martène, E., and Durand, U., *Veterum scriptorum et monumentorum historicorum . . . ,* 63
mathematics. *See* science and mathematics
medicine, Islamic influence, 154–55
Mediterranean, competition of East and West, 90–91. *See also* commerce
mercantile communes. *See* commerce (Mediterranean shipping) ; Italy
Michaud, J. F., 18, 20; analysis of chronicles in *Bibliothèque des croisades,* 60 ff
military orders, 143–46; Templars, 144–45; Hospitallers, 145–46
missions. *See* Mongols and missions
Mongols and missions, 134–36
Muḥammed. *See* Islam

Ottomans. *See* Counter-Crusade (Turkish) ; Islam

Palestine Pilgrims' Text Society Library, 47–52
Pennsylvania *History of the Crusades,* 23
philology, Islamic influence, 156
philosophy and theology, Islamic influence, 149–52
pilgrimage, 47–57, 109
Portuguese. *See* geography
propaganda, literature, 127–31

Records of Civilization (Columbia University) , 70–72
Recueil des Historiens des Croisades, 29–46
Reinaud, M., 35, 60, 69–70
Rhodes. *See* military orders (Hospitallers)
Riant, comte. *See* Société de l'Orient Latin
Roumania. *See* assises
Runciman, S., on sources for periods of Crusade, 25–26
Saint-Maur, Congrégation de, 19–20, 34–35, 64; *Histoire Littéraire de la France,* 19; Benedictines,

Saint-Maur *(Continued)*
19–20; Dom Berthereau, 19, 34–35
saints. *See* Constantinople; pilgrimage
Saladin, Arabic sources on life, 36–37, 51. *See also* Egypt and Syria (aftermath of Crusade)
science and mathematics, Islamic influence, 152–53
Société de l'Orient Latin, publications, 21
Spain. *See* Crusade histories; geography
Syria. *See* Egypt and Syria

Templars. *See* military orders
Turkey. *See* Counter-Crusade; Crusade histories; Islam

Venice, archives, 118. *See also* commerce (Mediterranean shipping)

war, art of, Islamic influence, 146–47
Wilken, E., 18
William of Tyre, life of, 17; work cited, 31

GLASGOW DEPARTMENT LIBRARIES UNIVERSITY
WITHDRAWN